Endorsements

"How can you resist a true story with the Kentucky Derby, the Cartel, Tijuana gambling, and a guy named Miami? You can't! Prepare yourself for the ride."

- Brandt Andersen, Executive Producer: *American Made* (2017), *Silence* (2016), and *Lone Survivor* (2013)

"I loved reading *The Greatest Gambling Story Ever Told* and couldn't put it down. It's a wonderfully stylish and entertaining story filled with action, suspense, and a lot of heart."

- Tobias Schliessler, ASC, Cinematographer of *Beauty and the Beast* (2017), *Dreamgirls* (2006), and *Lone Survivor* (2013)

"I loved the book and story! I usually don't like horse racing books because the writers don't typically understand racing. Mark has recreated the world's greatest racing event in an accurate, exciting, and intense portrayal. It's like being at the finish line with a million dollars on the line!"

- Aron Wellman, President & Founder of Eclipse Thoroughbred Partners, 25 Stakes Winners, and Winner of Belmont Stakes

"*The Greatest Gambling Story Ever Told* follows the development of champion Winning Colors through the eyes of her owner, trainer and jockey. But the drama is just beginning at the Tijuana Mexico betting windows, after Winning Colors wins the Kentucky Derby!"

- Steve Springer, Los Angeles Times award winning sportswriter and author of 11 books

D0556895

"An exciting story of a filly battling the males in the Kentucky Derby… and the gamblers that risked their lives on her. I was fascinated by the behind the scenes aspects of thoroughbred racing. A fun, fast, and exciting read."

- Ken Stovitz, Producer of *The Karate Kid* (1984)

"My wife read to me *The Greatest Gambling Story Ever Told* while I was driving with her from Washington to California. We were glued to the story as the miles rolled on and totally immersed in the characters as they shot off the pages with total realism. I felt like I knew the characters personally by the time we were a quarter of the way into the book. These three fun-loving buddies discover they placed a bet with the Mexican Cartel. Talk about a life-threatening problem that had us fearing for their lives. Putting the book down was not an option. My god it was intense and provided us with the fastest trip to Los Angeles ever! I wished there was a second book for the trip home. Mark Paul captured the audience and wrote a true page turner."

- Wallace Williams, Author of *Stand Down*,
The Candidates, and *Pay Back*

"I loved the story of the filly taking on the male colts and their chauvinistic trainers! It is incredibly exciting when she runs against them in the Derby. I loved the characters so much and I hated for the story to end."

- Patrice Scribante, Horse Lover

"These characters bet their lives on a 50 to 1 shot! The book is a fast paced read from cover to cover and the scenes getting out of Mexico scared me to death. These are some crazy gamblers betting on the world's greatest race. Loved it!"

- Richard Zien, Co-Founder, Mendelson and Zien Advertising

"I have been a Maître D' at the Santa Anita Turf Club for 42 years, and this wonderful book recreates the glory days of horse racing. I loved re-experiencing the story of the billionaire owners, famous trainers, and bold gamblers as they raced toward an epic Derby."

- Jimmy O'Hara, Maître D', Santa Anita Racetrack, 1977 to Present

"This booked ruined my vacation – because I sat in my room unable to stop reading! I was worried for the characters as they traveled to Mexico and back with millions in cash. I want to see this place in Tijuana, Mexico!"

- Rusty Weber, Wealth Manager

"I have owned horses for 30 years and loved this exciting and true story. The racing scenes will have you on the edge of your chair rooting for the brilliant filly battling the colts!"

- Joel Adelman, Thoroughbred Owner

"A fast, easy read with action that doesn't stop. I enjoyed the racing scenes as well as watching the foolhardy gamblers try to extract themselves from their predicaments. A thoroughly enjoyable read."

- Howard Parelskin, Attorney

"A wonderful and suspenseful journey on two guys taking the ultimate long shot bet. No hedges, no fallback, lots of potholes. An easy, fun read."

- Rick Edwards, Investor

"Three young American wild guys compete with the Mexican drug cartel and escaped with their lives. They have a great time with the ladies and lived to tell how they made a $1,000,000 killing betting on a filly and avoiding being killed themselves by the Mexican Cartel."

- Stephen Tow, Financial Advisor

THE GREATEST
GAMBLING
STORY
EVER TOLD

A TRUE TALE OF THREE GAMBLERS, THE KENTUCKY DERBY, AND THE MEXICAN CARTEL

MARK PAUL

The Greatest Gambling Story Ever Told
A True Tale of Three Gamblers, the Kentucky Derby, and the Mexican Cartel
By Mark Paul

1. BIO000000 2. BIO026000 3. GAM004040
Paperback ISBN: 978-1-949642-28-5
Hardcover ISBN: 978-1-949642-29-2
Ebook ISBN: 978-1-949642-30-8

Cover design by Lewis Agrell and JW Robinson

Printed in the United States of America

Authority Publishing
11230 Gold Express Dr. #310-413
Gold River, CA 95670
800-877-1097
www.AuthorityPublishing.com

DEDICATION

To my wife, partner, and love of my life who always believes in me, often for no apparent reason.

AUTHOR'S NOTE

The Greatest Gambling Story Ever Told is the colorful story of a spectacular three-year-old female racehorse in the male dominated world of thoroughbred racing. The book is a dramatic narrative of an exciting and frightening time in my life. It's based on personal experiences leading up to and during the Kentucky Derby. Hundreds of hours of research allowed me to portray and re-create the lives and actual events that occurred around the gamblers and participants in the running of this race. Occasionally places, persons, timelines, and details were changed to re-create events that occurred over three decades ago, and to protect identities and privacy. There are elements of creative nonfiction in this work (conversations were recreated) but it is based on events I witnessed or researched.

CONTENTS

Dedication vii

Author's Note ix

Chapter 1   Long Legged Lady 1

Chapter 2   Would You Bet Your Life on a 50-1 Shot? 28

Chapter 3   Cartel Trouble 40

Chapter 4   Stakes Class 49

Chapter 5   The Hotel Impala 60

Chapter 6   Girls Don't Belong. 68

Chapter 7   Heaven 79

Chapter 8   Newspaper Execution 97

Chapter 9   The Greatest Two Minutes 108

Chapter 10   Drug Dogs. 125

Chapter 11   Mariachi Madness 145

Photos. 148

Acknowledgements 159

Bibliography 161

About the Author 169

CHAPTER 1

Long Legged Lady

May 5, 1984, Churchill Downs Racetrack, Kentucky

A girl with long red hair, perhaps eight years old, was sitting high atop her father's shoulders, watching the horses load into the gate for the 110th running of the Kentucky Derby. They were standing in the packed grandstand at the stretch near the starting gate; nearly a quarter mile separated them and the finish line. She was holding a sign that read, "Beat the Boys! Althea!" She wanted to see a female horse win the prestigious race, something that a filly had accomplished only twice since 1875.

This filly, Althea, had drawn the dreaded rail post position. She was calm when she entered the gate. Althea was waiting behind the gate because 19 additional horses were still to be loaded into the starting gates, including another female. The other filly, Life's Magic, shared the same trainer as Althea: D. Wayne Lukas. The betting public believed the two fillies had a real chance; they were the favorites at odds of only 2.8-1, coupled in the wagering together.

After the outside gate, number 20, was loaded, the starter's bell rang and the gates sprung open!

The crowd of 126,000 fans roared as Althea broke just a bit slow, but recovered and frantically dug her hooves into the hard brown Kentucky soil, desperate to get in front of the other 19 charging horses. She was sprinting now, taking the lead running while on the inside part of the track near the white rail, past the fans, and into the first of the two long turns.

The red-haired girl's father yelled, "Althea's in front!"

She smiled and shouted, "Go girl! Go girl!"

A horse named Swale, a colt, was the one most expected to battle the favored Althea, (at 3-1 odds), and he settled just off the speeding filly on the lead as they charged into the turn at nearly 40 mph. With the sound of 80 hooves pounding into the track, all horses were seeking the immortality of a Derby win for their trainers and owners.

Althea now opened up on Swale by one-and-a-half lengths into the first left-handed turn.

The 71-year-old trainer of Swale was Woody Stephens of Kentucky, and like many successful older men, he had lost his politically correct filter some years before. Just that morning he had yelled to Lukas, "Dammit Wayne, keep your fillies out of my way."

"Althea won't be in your way, Woody. You'll have to catch her if you can."

"You're wasting your time. Keep the girls running against girls."

Lukas had been the first trainer in history to enter two fillies in the same Derby. He had been mocked and criticized by other trainers, the media, and many racing fans, for doing so, despite how Althea had defeated the colts in three other major stakes races already in her short career. To win a Derby requires a different type of horse—a horse that can race the classic distance of one-and-one-quarter miles and survive the long stretch run against the best horseflesh on the planet.

Just before the start of this race, a male fan yelled, "You're going to lose again Wayne…next year bring a colt!"

So far, in the 1984 Kentucky Derby, Lukas looked like a genius as Althea led the thundering pack into the backstretch. Hooves pounding, Swale and Althea were throwing back chunks of dirt into the faces of their nearest pursuers, nearly two lengths behind them. Swale began his attack on her outside right flank, challenging her for the lead. She felt his energy and dug in again, accelerating into the final turn, flatly refusing to yield to the larger colt on her outside. The huge raucous crowd had wagered $25,000,000 and the anticipated battle between the two betting favorites was on!

Now the red-haired girl could see the horses charging directly toward her position near the rail at the start of the stretch. "Come on, Althea! You can do it, girl!"

Swale was running easily under his champion jockey Laffit Pincay Jr. while Chris McCarron on Althea was furiously pumping his arms forward, urging the smaller filly to keep the battle going. She fought gamely to hold the second position as Swale rushed past, but the colts were making their ambitious stretch assaults now.

The other filly, Life's Magic, was caught in a wall of horses and making no impact.

Pincay, one of the most physically powerful riders in history, urged Swale forward with his piston-like arms, matching in exact rhythm the colt's giant strides as they surged away from the field.

Althea was spent from her early race speed. McCarron, feeling her fatigue beneath him, did not draw his whip. She lapsed to fifth, then 10th, then 15th, exhausted. At the wire, Althea beat only one horse that had been pulled up earlier in the race. She finished over 30 lengths behind the winning Swale and his celebrating trainer, Woody Stephens.

Lukas watched as Althea finish 19th after Life's Magic came in eighth. Despite winning 131 races, and smashing the all-time money won record for a single racing season, Lukas had failed for the sixth consecutive time in the world's most well-known horse race.

July 17, 1986, Keeneland Racetrack, Lexington, Kentucky

Two years after that race, the San Diego Chargers helmet logo stood tall on the tail of a gleaming private jet as it banked hard over Keeneland racetrack in Lexington, Kentucky. Trainer D. Wayne Lukas loved this part of horse racing—the private jets and traveling with billionaires who were committed to buying the best horseflesh in the world. Tall, lean, and fit, with gray hair and designer sunglasses, he looked every bit the Hollywood movie star. Many movie stars aren't tough, but Lukas was a former bareback bronco rodeo rider, and raced quarter horses as a jockey when young. He had been a rock-hard cowboy who came up through the ranks, training first on the rodeo circuit, and then the cheap track quarter horse circuit from the Midwest, to Texas, and then on to Southern California. He had spent years sleeping in the beds of pick-up trucks and shaving with cold water in front of side view mirrors. He had come from nowhere and now was the dominant thoroughbred racehorse trainer in the world.

Billionaire Eugene Klein was a man used to winning by playing aggressively and now competed with the best racehorse owners in the game, in the richest possible stakes races. In recent years, Klein had sold his Seattle SuperSonics NBA team, his San Diego Chargers NFL team, and his other considerable business interests to focus on a new passion—thoroughbred horseracing.

The private plane's flight attendants were former Chargers' cheerleaders who were stunning in their short skirts and white blouses. Both blonde and nearly as tall in heels as Lukas himself, they were used to being chatted up by passengers, but Lukas seemed not to notice them. Lukas was as handsome a guest as they had ever served, other than a few of the Chargers' players, and they tried to catch Lukas's attention. He was oblivious to their flirtations.

Lukas was looking to see what other private planes were already on the ground. As the plane taxied on the tarmac, Lukas pointed out to Klein some of the private jets owned by bidding competitors already on site. The largest of the jets dwarfed all the other planes. It belonged to sheik Mohammed bin Rashid al Maktoum, the defense minister of Dubai. Oil money was a different kind of money; it escalated competition at the horse auctions. The sheiks of Dubai who were also there were led by another horseman with the status of Lukas: the handsome and always impeccably dressed European, Robert Sangster. The sheiks were nicknamed The Doobie Brothers.

Also parked front and center on the tarmac was the jet of Greek shipping magnate Stavros Niachros. Stavros was born in Athens to a wealthy family, and by boldly investing $2,000,000 into a shipping business, he now was the richest magnate in the world. His personal history included four wives, each considerably younger than the first.

Lukas knew that this was going to be an epic Keeneland sales auction of prime horseflesh. He was out of his seat before the plane stopped, standing at the door, waiting for it to be opened. A man of immense energy, he was up at three a.m. every day to train and watch his horses. By five a.m., he was on the phone to his people in Florida, Kentucky, or Southern California, and all the other barns where he kept stables of the fastest racehorses in the world. At the auction today, he wanted to inspect the young horses on the block with his team of assistant trainers, bloodstock agents, and veterinarians who'd already been there for days evaluating the talent.

Only 14 years older than Lukas, Klein looked more like Lukas's father. Normally, Klein was considered a well-dressed man but next to Lukas he looked somewhat disheveled. Lukas could do that to anyone except Robert Sangster.

A private black Lincoln limousine carried Lukas and Klein down the long drive past the huge trees and white picket fences to the Keeneland Sales Pavilion, next to the historic Keeneland racetrack. The entrance to Keeneland is the most beautiful track entrance in America. The 1986 Keeneland auction was to open at 10:00 a.m., and the sales ring crowd was charged with excitement in a quiet, subdued way. The bidders were flush with hundreds of millions to bid. It was hard for these competitive rich men not to let themselves get carried away when bidding against other powerful rich men. The bidders were acutely aware that in just over a year some of these men would be standing in winners' circles accepting the trophies representing the richest, most prestigious stakes races in Kentucky, New York, California, and Florida. These billionaires were men at the top of their professions, and they were used to winning. They could afford to win and never planned on coming home empty handed. However, things can get complicated when bidding against the other richest men in the world. Often enough, a horse slips through an auction under the radar like the Triple Crown champion Seattle Slew—a racehorse that was sold for $17,500 as a yearling. No horse was going to be cheap today.

At 11:00 a.m. Lukas, wearing a freshly pressed white linen suit, rich blue tie, and white Stetson hat, opened the bidding on hip number 308 at $1,000,000, the highest opening bid ever recorded.

Robert Sangster smiled at Lukas and went up by an incredible incremental bid jump of $500,000. The bidding for one horse continued faster than Lukas had ever seen, with $500,000 being up bid every ten seconds: $3,000,000, now $5,000,000, now $8,000,000; and then the displayed bidding board stopped at $9,999,999 because it was out of digits and didn't go any higher.

The bids kept coming.

Klein had expected some competition, but not like this! His eyes were blinking rapidly, and he was afraid to move for fear he would be mistaken as bidding. "Who the hell are these guys?" he whispered to Lukas while remaining ramrod straight in his chair. "These guys have gold balls!"

The bidding was slowing now and only going up $50,000 per bid as Sangster competed against another secretive bidder that Klein could not even see. Finally, at $10,200,000 the gavel fell to Robert Sangster and his European buyers as the crowd cheered for the first time that morning.

Lukas as always looked polished, calm, and cool, but he knew he and Klein had to regroup, and fast. Lukas had a total budget of $8,000,000 from Klein and his other clients for the auction and quickly realized they could not go toe-to-toe with this new kind of insane oil money. Apparently, $8,000,000 was chump change for this group at the auction. Lukas had recognized this possibility long before the sale and told Klein quietly under his breath, "Go to Plan B."

Lukas knew the Europeans and the sheiks wanted proven classic winning bloodlines with colts they could breed as stallions for decades to come. But Klein and Lukas only cared about winning stakes races and purse money now; they didn't care if they did it with colts or fillies… or goats. If the horse looked like it could run, they were going to bid, especially if the horse was female and for sale under $300,000.

Lukas and Klein had not been born to money like the sheiks and other heirs to fortunes who were playing here with money from their parents' estates, and they were steadfastly committed to beating both the Arabs and the swells at their own rich man's game. The blue-blooded Kentucky owners and wealthy Arabs did not like the brash, tall, Jewish billionaire from Beverly Hills who was trying to invade their private club accompanied by the fast talking, slick suited Lukas. Let the auction competition continue!

Lukas had learned something valuable in his early years as a quarter horse trainer, sleeping in his pick-up truck and training horses on the cheap, rock bottom level racing circuits in Texas, Arizona, and Oklahoma. At these low-class, bottom purse level tracks, the horses ran in a straight line with their ears pinned back and flat out for 350 yards. In the quarter horse stakes races, the fillies regularly competed against and beat the colts head-to-head. Lukas believed strongly he could train thoroughbred fillies to run against the males and beat them in prestigious races, despite his being laughed at by the macho good-old-boys trainers' network from Los Angeles to New York. Despite failure with his two fillies in the 1984 Kentucky Derby, he believed a female could and would win that race again. Lukas had a proven eye for horseflesh, regardless if he was buying a $600 quarter horse, or a half a million dollar thoroughbred.

Suddenly there was commotion as a wild, tall, leggy, gray filly was led into the ring. She was not happy while being led out for display and wheeled around the auction stage trying to free herself from both her handler and the leather lead attached to her halter. Two additional horse handlers came forward trying to constrain her, and one made the mistake of grabbing hold of her left ear. She reared and kicked, striking a glancing blow to the third handler that sent him careening to the floor. He had seen enough of this damn horse, as earlier that morning he had witnessed her bite two older male stallions while being led to her holding pen.

The 1-year-old filly was not slim and trim like the other yearling females that had daintily pranced in all day like they were stepping in snow. This gray filly was built more like a tall version of Mike Tyson, with dappled hindquarters that showed muscles like an older stallion. Lukas noticed she was pulling her handler around wherever she decided to go, not where he was trying to lead her.

She grunted loudly and violently threw her head to the side, pulling her handler completely off his feet as he was trying to hold on to the bridle of this huge and spirited animal. The bidding on her opened at $100,000 and Klein told Lukas to go to $250,000. When the bid reached $300,000, Klein gave Lukas the signal to keep going, $350,000, $400,000, then $500,000 and finally to $575,000. Lukas had told Klein she was Lukas's top-rated filly in the entire sale and both men were ecstatically high-fiving each other when the gavel fell. The purchase of Winning Colors ended their auction and Klein sprinted out of the pavilion to call his wife Joyce, excited to tell her about the last filly they had just bought for $575,000 by outbidding the oil money rich Arabs.

Joyce asked, "How much did you pay for an unraced 1-year-old filly?"

"Five hundred seventy-five thousand," Klein said, and then paused. "Yes, honey, we went way over budget...but hell, buying horses was your idea. I want you to be happy!"

Young 2-year-old thoroughbred fillies don't have testosterone running through their veins making them big and often stupid like their brothers. Just walking down the shed row, colts will prove they are born different than their sisters. They dart their heads out of their stalls to play by biting faces, hands, or any other extremity within reach. Their sisters usually nuzzle up to their grooms and handlers, playfully prodding to get more carrots or just to get rubs and affection.

Winning Colors was different. She would physically intimidate her grooms and especially the other horses around her, regardless of their sex or age. She was high strung and when someone tried to put a halter on her, she would rear back and threaten to kill them. Eventually her handlers learned to put on the halter disassembled, and then put it back together after it was slipped over her head.

As she aged, Winning Colors filled in with even more muscle. She was so tall, seasoned horsemen in the barn couldn't believe she wasn't a grown, older, male racehorse. Now a 2-year-old, Winning Colors looked like a 4-year-old mature, full-grown male.

Barn of D. Wayne Lukas at Santa Anita Racetrack, May 1986

In May 1986, Lukas called one of his young grooms, Luis Palos, into his private office. The 25-year-old groom had been with Lukas for two years now and was a smart, hard-working, polite, and quiet young man from Mexico City. Luis came to work on time in clean blue jeans and polished cowboy boots. His jet-black hair was neatly trimmed and combed.

Luis was worried. He had never been called into señor Lukas's private office, and feared he was to be let go. He said, "Hola, señor."

Lukas shook his hand and looked him straight in the eye for three seconds. "Luis...I like you. I've been watching you. You come in early every day. You look sharp and work hard."

"Gracias, señor."

"I have a filly for you. She's special. She needs someone like you. I want you to personally take care of her...Winning Colors."

Luis smiled. He wasn't being fired. He'd been chosen to work with the big filly. "Si, I know her. Ella es la gran potra [filly]. Posiblemente...a little...dangerous."

Lukas laughed, "Yes, that's the one. She's your responsibility now. You take good care of her, Luis...and you can make more money. I need you to travel with her, too. I know you have a wife and three children. Can you go on airplanes with her? You will be going to New York with her soon."

"Si, señor. My wife can watch mis niños...no problema."

With that, Luis was personally assigned one of the most promising young horses in a stable of over 200 horses. Since Santa Anita racetrack in Southern California was their home base, Luis knew Lukas would check in on him multiple times per day. But he also knew he could advance his career, and one day, perhaps become an assistant trainer and stop having to perform the daily hard manual labor required of a groom. Luis was being paid $6.25 per hour, $2 over minimum wage, to care for a 2-year-old horse now worth over $1,000,000.

Luis treated her like she belonged to him, even making his wife, Mariana, pack special treats in his lunch pail to give to the filly every day. He was known to have said, "If I don't bring her food every day she will kill me! Really.... She will kill me!"

On his first day with Winning Colors, Luis had made the mistake of grabbing her by the ear. She violently threw her head into him, giving him a black eye and bloody lip. Luis learned not to let anyone, ever, touch her ears. He feared for anyone who got too close to her, as they could get hurt, and, injure her in the process. Winning Colors only let Luis touch her anywhere near her head, and the stablehands learned to always have Luis present to calm her down when the veterinarians or blacksmiths came to work on her racing plates (shoes) and hooves.

He was tender with her, and she learned to trust him. She relaxed when he spoke to her. He nicknamed her Mamacita.

Luis liked working for Lukas because he loved the horses—but not the hours. At most barns, the day would start early at 4:30 or 5:00 a.m., but for the Lukas barn, it started at 3:30 a.m.

The other barns would start with the assistant trainers, grooms, and hot walkers trying to get warm around the coffee pot, but the Lukas barn allowed no coffee pot distraction. Lukas had a worker every day that just groomed the ground while following every man, woman, and horse around to rake the footprints into a special, Lukas-selected fan pattern in the dirt. The trainer Willard Proctor had been quoted as saying of Lukas, "I don't know if he can train a horse…but he sure can landscape."

The Lukas barn looked like a Four Seasons Hotel compared to the other barns, always with fresh flowers planted everywhere and D. Wayne Lukas logos all over the stable blankets, trucks, water buckets, flowerpots, horse halters, saddles, t-shirts, hats, and jackets around the barn. His assistant trainers teased Lukas, "Where's the gift shop?" Lukas would occasionally send stablehands home if they reported to work in dirty clothes. But the men and woman working there knew that like a Special Forces unit of the US Marines, they were the best in the business, and everyone in horseracing knew the Lukas barn was the best in the nation.

The track's horses and trainers are typically located behind the tracks and are referred to as backstretch workers. At every racetrack in the nation, these workers are very similar. The tracks have acres and acres filled with hard-working men and women, mostly from Latin American countries like Mexico and Guatemala. The trainers and the owners are the bosses, the horses and the jockeys are the stars, but the labor and skill required to care for the horse population in the backstretch stables falls on the backs of these people.

Workdays often exceed 12 hours, whether under the blistering sun of Texas, or the freezing cold mornings of New York, or New Jersey. The cleaning of barns, walking mile after mile with the prized horses to cool them down after workouts, feeding, bathing, and caring for the health of each equine athlete requires a staff that has the right expertise. The racehorses are big, powerful, and often unpredictable; only experienced horse people can co-exist with the animals. Nearly every backstretch worker can tell stories of being bitten or kicked. The backstretch workers travel the circuit from racetrack to racetrack throughout the year, leading a nomadic life in often close to poverty conditions that bring their communities into very close friendships.

A top horse can be worth $5,000,000 or more, but even an above-average thoroughbred at a top track can earn $40,000 or more in prize money per year. The experienced and dependable grooms and workers can be just as important to the success of a fragile racehorse as the trainer, and the staff becomes emotionally attached to the fast, beautiful animals in their care twenty-four hours per day.

Luis traveled everywhere with Winning Colors. The short trips were easier; cross-country trips were more difficult. After their first flight from Santa Anita to the historic Saratoga racetrack in New York, Luis often stayed with Mamacita in the barn at night, even though he was off the clock. Although he was tending a beloved animal, Luis spent time thinking of his wife and children, 3,000 miles away and in their own beds.

The racing calendar has seasons, as the track circuit venues change about every three months. The biggest race meets of the entire year are held at the three spa tracks that are summer retreats for the wealthy: Del Mar racetrack in San Diego, California, Keeneland Racetrack in Lexington, Kentucky, and the famous Saratoga Racetrack, a three-hour drive north of New York City. The most expensive, best-bred horses in the country were all pointed to the top stakes races each summer at these exclusive venues. Winning Colors was ready to make her debut on the Saratoga stage, at the grandest of racetracks, against the best and most expensive young fillies in training.

August 13, 1987, Saratoga Racetrack, New York

Before he left California, Luis promised his wife he would stop betting on the horses. She'd noticed his meager take-home pay was often far less than it should be. He hoped Mariana wouldn't look in the box in the closet where they kept their savings because he'd bet all they had on her on the day Mamacita was making her debut. He told all his fellow workers, "She is the one," as he'd personally wagered $900.

The race wouldn't be easy, as a full field of 11 top young fillies were competing against the tall gray filly. Despite not being the morning line favorite when printed in the race day program, the word was out on her ability, as she had opened in the Saratoga third race betting at 6-1 but was now bet down to the solid fan favorite at just under 2-1. Luis was smiling like a proud father as he led her under halter around the enormous infield paddock in the front of the Saratoga track. Winning Colors' local jockey, Randy P. Romero, was shocked to see the size of the massive filly when he met her in the saddling area.

Luis told the jockey, "Just hold on and don't fall off…she will do the rest, amigo, I promise…and if you fall off, you owe me $900."

The other eight well-bred fillies were led to the starting gate for the one-turn, seven- furlong race (each furlong is one-eighth of a mile) adorned in their bright colored racing silks from the stables of other wealthy owners and their top ranked national trainers. Many of the other fillies were sweating in the August New York heat and humidity, but Winning Colors appeared cool and dry.

On the way to the post, Winning Colors lunged at two other competitors, a game she liked to play. The huge metal starting gate is a frightening beast to young racehorses, but Winning Colors, in her yellow and blue colors, calmly entered stall number three and stood rock still, as the other 10 fillies loaded. When the starting gate bell rang, the gates snapped opened, and Winning Colors nearly pulled Romero's legs out of the saddle irons with her acceleration. In 10 strides, she was a half-length in front of the field while battling two other well-bred and well-bet fillies sprinting down the backstretch.

Thoroughbred horseraces are carefully timed into quarter-mile segments. As each quarter of a mile is completed, the elapsed time is posted on the television monitors and on the tote board, located in the center of the track, which also displays the horses' current betting odds. Each quarter-mile segment is usually run in around 24 seconds, but the first quarter-mile is usually run faster than the later quarter-mile segments of the dirt races, as the horses become tired in the later stages of the race.

Races are usually run at distances from three-quarters-of-a-mile (one-turn sprints), up to one-and-one-quarter miles (two-turn routes) for races like the Kentucky Derby. Top racehorses can run nearly 40 mph, but don't go full speed for an entire race as they must reserve their energy for the later parts of the race and hold off the late charging "closers" at the finish. The finish line is often called "the wire," as a wire runs overhead to assist the photo finish camera. Younger (2- and 3-year-old) racehorses are not nearly as fast as mature racehorses, aged four to seven.

Female horses of all ages, like humans, usually run several seconds slower than their male counterparts over the course of a race. Winning Colors was proving to be the exception. As a 2-year-old filly, she was now cruising at a blistering 22-and-one-fifth second first quarter-mile pace—a fast pace for a seasoned older horse, and incredibly fast for a 2-year-old female.

During the race, Romero was trying to reserve her speed and save energy for the long home stretch, known as the Graveyard of Champions. The Saratoga racetrack stretch leading to the finish line is long and tiring to horses, and many a well bet, well regarded, previous champion horse had tired and lost their good lead in the stretch run for home. Winning Colors was flying out on the lead, bounding away from the other fillies with each of her huge strides. She was going full out and entered the left-hand stretch turn one-and-one-half lengths in front, as the other fillies made their charging moves, but she was now hitting her full speed. She'd decisively opened by four lengths over her closest pursuer, exited the turn, and took dead aim for the wire. She darted a bit to her left in the stretch run, nearly scraping the white paint off the inner rail with her gray body. The pursuing jockeys were whipping and yelling encouragement to their fillies, trying to catch the flying Winning Colors, but they were doing so in vain.

She wasn't just beating the field; she was embarrassing them. At the finish line 1,000 feet away, Luis was red-faced, jumping up and down, shouting at the top of his lungs, "Go Mamacita! Go Mamacita!"

Jockey Romero took hold of her near the wire, tucked his unused whip away, having never asked her to fully extend herself. Winning Colors coasted home in front of the second-place horse by nearly three lengths at the wire, with the rest of the field strewn back nearly 20 lengths behind. Luis was running around the track holding his tickets high to the sky and yelling, "Si!...Si!...Si!...Si! Esa es mi chica!"

Soon there would be $2,700 in the box in the closet of Luis and Mariana Palos.

August 17, 1987, Rancho Santa Fe, California

Later in the week after the race, D. Wayne Lukas and Eugene Klein met in San Diego to discuss race plans for Winning Colors as they now knew they had something very special in the tall and feisty filly. They flew her back by private jet and bedded her down back at her home Santa Anita racetrack, 17 miles east of Los Angeles.

Lukas was not known for patience with horses and was often criticized for running his young horses too often. However, he was being especially patient with his new promising starlet. He chose to wait from August to the end of December to run her again at Santa Anita.

Top horses can occasionally capture the imagination of the American public the way Seabiscuit, Seattle Slew, or Secretariat did, but the problem is that a horse's racing career is short. Most top ranked horses today race two to four times at age two, five to eight races at age three, and another five to eight races at age four. Typically, top stakes horses are retired after age four when their breeding value is high, compared to the limited purse income they can win while racing. By the time the horse is a recognized star at age three after winning a Derby or other top high-profile stakes race, the horse probably has less than another 18 months to race before a life of retirement. The horse's fame is so short-lived that a true fan base cannot be easily developed. A comparative top human athlete such as an NFL quarterback, or Major League Baseball pitcher or hitter, will typically have a 10- to 15-year career playing their sport, but the careers of the four-legged stars are short lived. The animals themselves typically live into their 20s but race only a few years of their lives.

At the age of 25, jockey Gary Stevens was just three years removed from a coma that left him unconscious for 16 hours after slamming into the Santa Anita rail. It was a frightening training accident that was caught on video in all its gruesome detail. For many months, his speech pattern was impacted. Upon regaining consciousness, he learned that his right knee was nearly destroyed, and his promising career likely was over. Stevens was quoted as saying he did not fear being on a horse's back and resumed riding in six months. In many ways, the biggest stars in horseracing are the jockeys. Stevens, Idaho born, with boyish good looks and a smile to charm the ladies, was becoming a Southern California favorite among the race fans.

Jockeys who avoid career-ending injuries can race for many decades. This career longevity is made far more difficult because the jockeys, including their saddle, clothing, and whip, must weigh less than 114 pounds on race day. As the jockeys mature, like most humans, they usually thicken and gain weight. Stories of jockeys eating, then purging, are typical for the vocation.

Bill Shoemaker was still racing strong at 57 years of age, and still an elite rider 45 years into his career. Most of the US top jockeys come from the same Latin American countries as the backstretch workers and are a tough-as-leather, fearless group of mostly men. Stevens was unique among top riders as he was American born. As American as apple pie, Stevens was handsome and easy for US fans to relate to. He began his riding career at age 12 by convincing his dad to put him on quarter-mile sprint racehorses. His older brother Scott was a top jockey and had refused to ride a crazy horse named Little Star because of her history of flipping over and trying to pin the jockeys under her. When Scott refused to ride the crazed animal, Gary stepped up to ride Little Star, and went on to be a leading rider in Seattle. Scott became like a coach for Gary and taught him the nuances of race riding.

Being a racehorse is dangerous but being the jockey on the horse's back is far more perilous. Racehorses run at high speeds for short bursts, yet horses' ankles are smaller than a human's ankles, and must support the 1,000-pound charging animal. A top, seasoned jockey may race as many as six or eight races per day, five days per week, totaling nearly 1,500 races per year. A rider falls during a thoroughbred race about every 500 rides, so the statistics indicate that an active top jockey will hit the ground about three times per year.

Stevens had become a leading rider for Lukas by overcoming his traumatic injuries, and because of his talent and hard work. He rode hurt in 1986 and early 1987, still not fully recovered from the Santa Anita accident, but now was finally riding fully fit and healthy. Not yet a star, Stevens was a rising young talent, and was a leading rider at the Southern California race meetings held at Hollywood Park, Del Mar, and Santa Anita. Lukas liked to hire him, and he was a favorite of Klein for his personal stable.

One morning he told his brother Scott, "You can't imagine what it is like to ride for Mr. Klein. He sends limousines for me to come to his ranch. And, my God, you should see his private jet! He never lets me fly commercial when I ride his horses at other tracks. Brother, we are from Idaho and now it's the big time!"

Scott as always was happy for his little brother's success. He knew how hard it had been for Gary to achieve this level of racing achievement. He had watched Gary at age seven be diagnosed with Legg-Calve-Perthes syndrome, a degenerative disease which destroys the hip socket joint, requiring him to wear a metal brace for 19 months. Gary's first attempt to break into the ultra-competitive Southern California jockey colony had been a disaster; he'd won only four races in 90 attempts. Lukas and Klein had changed his life, yet he remained humble and aware a jockey's life is a fragile existence. Stevens had only one weakness at the track and that was his penchant for fighting with other jockeys after races. If he could control his temper, and not be suspended, his future was bright. He just needed one special horse to prove his talent.

December 27, 1987, Santa Anita Racetrack, California

Modern thoroughbreds are considered much more fragile now than their predecessors were 50 years ago. For instance, in 1935, the famous

Seabiscuit raced 35 times just as a 2-year-old. By comparison, this next race would be Winning Colors' second and final start as a 2-year-old. Trainers in the 1920s and 1930s believed running 2-year-olds hard and often made them stronger and better able to handle the rigorous demands of racing when they became mature racehorses. Horses of that era were no doubt sounder and sturdier than the ones that run today. If a trainer were to do that in modern racing, they would be chastised and called cruel.

A horse with a five-month layoff between races is usually considered one of the worst wagers at the track, but Winning Colors' handlers who were with her every day knew she was unusual—so big, fast, and physical for a young horse. She could cruise easily at such a high speed that the daily exercise riders would find their hands worn to the point of bloody and raw by trying to control her in the morning workouts. Now four-and-a-half months since her sparkling race debut she was ready for her second start.

Lukas was becoming known as a "ladies' man" due to his incredible recent stakes race winning successes with the female horses in his care. Now to close out her 2-year-old season this cool and crisp late December day in California, Winning Colors was racing against five other promising fillies, including several that had shown to be extremely fast in their morning workouts. Winning Colors had drawn the most undesirable post position possible in the number one post, located down next to the inner fence, and this fact worried Lukas. The rail post position can especially bother precocious, young, unseasoned horses that often shy away from being squeezed down inside by horses charging alongside them on their right flank. If the rail horse breaks even a half-step slow, the other horses can come over and squeeze it against the fence, forcing the horse to run around outside the field to have any chance of prevailing.

Lukas told Stevens before the race, "She is like a storm…she can seem peaceful and relaxed…but anything can set her off and she becomes a maniac. Keep her away from noise and commotion or you will be sitting on a tornado. She is big and tough but also very fragile."

Winning Colors was staying focused as she calmly entered the gate, just as in New York, like a more seasoned veteran racehorse with years of experience. The other horses were jostling and banging against their gates as their Hispanic jockeys yelled to the starter to wait: "Espere! Espere!" as they worked to get their wild fillies settled and straight in the gate for the break.

The track announcer's voice came over the public address system, "The flag is up!" The horses were fully loaded and ready for the start when the starting bell clanged and the gates popped open.

Winning Colors exploded out of the gate with powerful long strides into the short three-quarter mile, one-turn race. The other fillies could not keep up with the big gray rockets early speed and she was in front by two-and-a-half lengths in under five seconds, increasing her margin every second. Gary Stevens was along for the ride she gave, sitting still on her back, never pushing her for more run. She was setting a fast pace—a pace only before seen in the top older, seasoned male sprinters in the nation. There was a problem with her 21-and-four-fifths-of-a-second as well as her 44-and-four-fifths-of-a-second opening fractions for the first quarter and half-mile. She was running too fast, too soon. A racehorse cannot sustain a flat-out pace like that for an entire race without tiring down the stretch. She was not conserving her energy—something that's often called "rating." She was running in a crazy exhibition of speed.

Stevens was trying his best to ration her energy. He explained later, "I didn't know she was going so insanely fast. She was doing it easily, not running off with me."

Winning Colors was able to run at a pace not seen by young fillies, and she was doing it effortlessly. She lengthened her body and led the field of six horses down the long Santa Anita backstretch with her long strides and gray mane flying in the wind while the other jockeys were desperate in urging their mounts to make a charge and cut into her lead. Winning Colors must have sensed she had no competition from the other young fillies.

As Stevens was trying to get her to slow her pace down and reserve energy for the stretch challenges, she did relax without pouring on her full energy and slowed to a still quick, but more sensible pace. She cruised into the sweeping left-hand turn leading by three-and-a-half lengths.

When they straightened for home, Stevens let the reins out a notch, chirped to her, and she responded by digging into the ground with her front hooves and pulling forward in long strides. The other fillies were way behind. The finish line approached, and she drifted to her left, nearly touching the inner rail. Stevens looked back and could see no closing threat. As she cruised to the wire, Stevens grabbed the reins 100 yards out to slow her down and save more energy.

Winning Colors won by four lengths. Easy.

Her groom Luis was again standing at the rail, hands held high with a thick stack of winning mutual tickets yelling, "Si!...Si!...Si!...Si! Esa es mi chica!"

Trainers, grooms, and backstretch workers will tell you horses know when they win a race. They carry themselves differently after a win, or a loss. Winning Colors was fully in her element as she cantered down the backstretch while being cooled out. She refused to be pulled up for her jockey. She was in such a state of joy after being allowed to release her stored energy that she did not want to stop running. Stevens later told Lukas, "She could've run another race that day. She was not even breathing hard after the race and could not blow out a candle if placed under her nose."

The Kleins's preferred turf club table was located above the finish line, and they erupted in screams of joy as their expensive filly charged to victory. All six of them marched triumphantly down the three flights of stairs to the winner's circle, to get their pictures taken with the happy, shining, tall gray filly.

After dismounting, Stevens told his fellow jockey Jacinto Vasquez, "That horse has attitude. I'm going to win the Kentucky Derby on that filly."

Vasquez raised an eyebrow. Stevens had never spoken like that about any horse to him. He told Stevens, "You don't know what it takes to win a Derby."

Stevens loved her fiery, precocious attitude, and her amazing athleticism, even if she was high-strung and difficult to control. The two were a good match together, fearless, with a will to win and take chances. They didn't run for second money, but gunned to the front, defying any equine or human athlete to keep pace with them.

Eugene and Joyce Klein and a boisterous group of champagne-drinking friends celebrated Winning Colors' win at an elegant candlelit French dinner. Joyce smiled, noticing her husband was as happy as she had seen him in years.

He was telling one of his favorite stories: "After the games, Howard Cosell bugged me all the damn time to ride in my jet. That's the last thing I needed is Cosell in my plane for five damn hours. Joyce was always scolding me for the way I talked to the media, telling me, 'Honey, you need to think more before you talk to the press.' But one week later he asks me again...and I tell Howard that it's only a small plane and we've got a limited supply of oxygen to get us all the way back to California. It worked...he didn't ask again!"

His companions asked him why he sold the football team.

Klein's eyes met his wife's, and they both looked away. Then Klein explained: "Did I tell you about my Chargers' players after the '82 Miami playoff game? I gave the players my goddamn beautiful airplane to fly home from the game. How did they repay my generosity? One of them brought a kilo of cocaine back on my plane to sell. My plane! After that, the FBI was investigating me for drug trafficking. They could have confiscated and kept my jet! The players didn't even try to hide the drugs. No, the stupid asses started to cut it up and began putting the coke up their noses on the plane, in front of the stewardesses! I said, 'To hell with football players! Let's go buy some horses. Horses don't deal coke!'"

Joyce Klein knew her 65-year-old husband was not the retiring type, and after selling the San Diego Chargers, she encouraged him to relax at the racetrack. In typical Eugene Klein fashion, he immediately told her to find him the best horse trainer in the world. D. Wayne Lukas had come to Klein's house the same week Joyce called, and maneuvered his new Rolls Royce up the long impressive estate driveway to the Klein's Rancho Santa Fe home, located just north of San Diego. Lukas was wearing a $3,000 David Rickey navy blue pinstripe suit and as always looked like he should be playing James Bond in the movies, not training horses in dusty stables. Lukas had over 200 custom sports jackets and suits in his closet and dressed better working in the barn than other trainers did in the turf club dining room.

Upon meeting Lukas, Klein had been at first put off by the slick clothes and fancy car, but quickly found him fascinating because of his fast-talking but brutally honest persona, with enough energy to run the Sun.

Klein said to him, "I didn't know horse trainers drove such fancy rigs."

Lukas replied, "I said I wasn't going to cheat you. I didn't say I was going to work for nothing."

"Why should I give you my horses to train?"

Lukas told him a story. "During a race another trainer had a horse get squeezed on the inside rail. The horse got bumped so bad he flipped over the inside rail, landing in a deep puddle of water. The horse drowned. When the horse owner called the trainer to ask how his horse ran that day, he had to say, 'Not so good, he drowned.'" Lukas laughed and then said, "Mr. Klein I may not be the best trainer in the world...but not one of my horses has ever drowned. I already have more horses in training than any other trainer in the country, and I don't need more owners. I need the right owners. I mean serious owners that are not afraid to spend real money and try to win the country's biggest races, like the Derby, and the Breeders' Cup. I need big boys to think and play big, and I know we can do it, because I'm the leading trainer in the country already. I am a winner, and I will make you money by racing champions, and breeding champions."

After surviving two coronary bypass operations in his sixties, and after spending millions of dollars on a pro football team with players he couldn't understand or relate to, Klein was now playing in the thoroughbred fast lane, with the gutsiest trainer in the world. As a former bomber navigator in World War II, he had faced live action from enemy anti-aircraft guns, and fighter pilots. Klein was a gambler at heart. He had gambled his money to buy a pro football team, and he was now investing in the fastest thoroughbreds that could be bought.

He also knew he was running out of time.

That same Sunday, December 27, 1987, during the night, Luis and two of his other backside racetrack buddies from the Lukas barn, Rafael and Ruben, took their two days off and headed their beat up, old, red pick-up truck onto a long road into the desert for their first trip to Las Vegas. They believed in Luis's undefeated Mamacita after her two stunning victories and were committed to bet on her to win the 1988 Kentucky Derby at the Caesars Palace future book venue.

The race was still five months away, held as always on the first Saturday in May, and Louisville, Kentucky, was 2,000 miles away from Mamacita's current California stall. But, the odds in future book wagering are affected by how early a wager is made. For instance, you can bet on the possible outcome of a future US Presidential election four years, three years, or even one month before it happens. But if you bet early, when there is more uncertainty as to the eventual result, the odds offered are fixed dramatically higher than they are just before the event. For Luis and friends, Winning Colors still was an unlikely long shot to even run in the Derby against the best males in the country, and if she didn't run in, and win the Derby, their future bet money would not be refunded. Luis didn't care, and he told his buddies, "Amigos, I will take care of her like she belongs to me. Do not worry."

They thought he was perhaps just a little loco, but he was so passionate in his belief in her ability, they couldn't say no. Luis watched her every day train alongside other top racehorses, and she always passed them when she pleased, even against the older males.

The friends stayed outside of the Las Vegas Strip at an inexpensive, $39-per-night motel room, sharing one room with two queen beds. Their average day's pay at the barn was less than $50 each, but Klein had handed Luis a $500 tip after her race that day and told him to share it with the other stablehands who'd worked with Winning Colors. That $500 and all the other money they could scrape together was stuck in Luis's boot. That night they ate at an inexpensive Mexican restaurant and took two six-packs of beer to the small pool outside their room, where they sat up until two a.m. listening to Latin music and getting buzzed. They could see the glimmering lights of the Strip a mile away in the cold, windy, desert winter night but could not afford to get involved with the gambling, girls, and other attractions.

"We are a long way from home, my friends," Luis said to his work buddies.

Rafael asked, "Where is home? Are you glad you left Mexico, amigo?"

Luis replied, "Home is here…and there too. Of course, I am glad… and thankful. Tonight my children are safe…and fed…and warm, with their mother."

Rafael said, "You have to get up every day at three a.m. and work. Lukas is a ball buster. He sent me home because I was dressed too dirty. Then I clean up after his horses."

"Remember when we didn't have work? I'm happy to work. Lukas is a pain in the ass sometimes…but he works hard, too. Like he never sleeps. Let's get my filly home in the Derby, amigos…then I will buy a house for my niños and Mariana…with a pool!"

"A groom with a pool…you think you are a rich man?"

"Maybe…maybe."

The next day they slept until 7:30 a.m., which seemed like a late morning to them after working at the Lukas barn. They pulled themselves together, cleaned up, and put on their best jeans, brass belt buckles, plaid shirts, boots, and large cowboy hats. Then they feasted on platters of the huevos rancheros breakfast special and drank two pitchers of black coffee at a Denny's restaurant near the Las Vegas Strip.

"Let's go make some dinero," Luis said to his track buddies as they packed up their pick-up truck and headed straight to valet parking at the lobby of the Caesars Palace casino. The sign above advertised "Tom Jones Live" and they asked each other, "Quien es Tom Jones?"

The three men were focused on their gambling mission, avoiding the slot machines, craps, and blackjack tables on their way straight to the sprawling Sports and Race Book at the back of the casino's floor. The walls of the betting mecca were covered with banks of television monitors the size of king beds, but there was not much activity on a Monday morning before noon. Luis asked the bartender how much for a beer. When he heard it was $2.75, he gave up being thirsty for one. They found the printed sheets for the 1988 Kentucky Derby in a far corner of the race book and located her name and odds toward the end of the sheet: "Winning Colors: 100-1."

Rafael said, "These gringos are estúpido. Let's take their money!"

The three found the one open betting window. After working to communicate in English with the bookmaker, Luis handed over the Derby printed odds sheet while pointing to their circled choice. Then he reached down into his cowboy boot for their shared bankroll. "Two-thousand dolares, por favor."

The ticket writer at the window had to call for a supervisor because although $2,000 wasn't a huge bet for one of the largest casinos in Nevada, the casino's exposure was still $200,000 if Winning Colors were to win the Derby; significant to even the Caesars Palace Race and Sports Book. The bookmaker printed the ticket and handed it to the men saying, "Good luck."

They retrieved their old but clean pick-up truck from the valet parking attendant, tipped the kid one dollar, and headed back to Santa Anita racetrack, five hours away, going right to the barn that evening to see their girl, Luis's Mamacita, Winning Colors.

Winning Colors' growing racing fan base didn't have long to wait to get excited, as Lukas was now ready to ramp up his big plans for her 1988 campaign. All racehorses have the same birthday, turning one year older, every January first. If a horse is born in December, it still turns a year old on January first. Winning Colors, born March 14, 1985, was now a 3-year old and ready to be tested in her first stakes race at Santa Anita. This would be her first longer race, around two turns. Many professional gamblers were still somewhat skeptical that any horse with that much blazing early speed could ration (rate) her energy over a longer distance with two turns, and still hold off the closers in the stretch run. Winning Colors had shown unbelievable sprinting speed but had yet to show she could be controlled by a jockey over a longer race.

Every year there are dozens of horses that get Derby hype because they win short sprint races, in fast times, and by large margins. As these horses mature, the stakes races are run at longer and more demanding distances, and their breeding comes into play. Most cheaply bred horses cannot stretch their speed to win at even a one-mile distance, yet alone the demanding one-and-one-quarter-mile classic distance of the Kentucky Derby.

As Kentucky Derby race contenders attempt to advance toward the world's most famous race each May, they are challenged to race longer distances, against tougher stakes, and quality competition. Most will fall short, and be dropped down into lower class races, offering smaller purse money, while racing against horses of similar speed, not of Triple Crown stature. It is a process of elimination done every spring, starting with over 40,000 thoroughbred horses foaled. Only the best 20 or less horses qualify to make it into the Kentucky Derby starting gate for just one to emerge victorious.

The racing season is always changing because of the beautiful and constant unveiling of new equine talent. At the start of each year, the newly turned 3-year-olds strive to qualify for the Triple Crown races. Handicappers look to catch lightning in a bottle by ferreting out the possible Derby entrants, at long odds, before the horses become well-known stars, and then they are bet down to low odds in the many Derby prep races.

"Who is your Derby horse?" is a constant question on the backstretch, months before the race is run. After the Triple Crown races, consisting of the Kentucky Derby, Preakness, and Belmont are completed, the summer action shifts to the baby races, consisting of the new 2-year-olds that are just making their initial career starts. As the late spring days lengthen into summer, the big handicap stakes races are run for older horses, for massive purses.

In the fall, the action shifts to the Breeders' Cup championship races with total purses exceeding $10,000,000. These races determine the Eclipse Awards for the best horses in each division, 2-year-old, sprinters, 3-year-old, turf (grass) racing, and older champions. The races and awards are broken down between the sexes, with females seldom asked to run against the males. Now, the now maturing 3-year-olds must step up and face the older horses to win the stakes money offered. The horses change track circuits for variety. It is a yearly cycle of life that horse players enjoy, and they watch it play out in the magnificent racing venues.

Winning Colors was no longer a racetrack secret, and the fans bet on her so heavily she was the 3-5 odds on favorite in the one-mile La Centinela Stakes for newly turned 3-year-olds. The race came up with less competition than she had previously faced, as it was run as the

Wednesday feature race against seven other fillies. As Gary Stevens loaded her into the gate, he knew his job was to win the race, and to school the young filly. He had to teach her to rate and ration her brilliant speed to hold some in reserve for the late challenges that would be coming from horses that had conserved their energy for decisive late bids, in the longer races to come. Klein and Lukas now had over 100 horses in training together, and only a few would likely become champions. These horses first must be tested and culled out to see which had the heart, talent, and ability to run fast over the longer distances required of the top-stakes caliber horses.

Winning Colors was deemed one of the brightest prospects in the barn, and Lukas had his son Jeff take over the day-to-day training plans of the rising star. Jeff personally checked on her throughout the day, and made sure Luis had everything she could possibly need. Jeff told Luis, "We both know she's special. Just focus on the gray, Luis. Full time...all the time. If anyone complains, tell them to see me."

"Si, señor. I will...like she is mine!"

Luis had his work cut out for him. Winning Colors was becoming feistier all the time. It was around this time that Gary Stevens told a reporter, "The safest place to be around Winning Colors was on her back."

She was like a young male stud—so powerful that she required a high level of training and racing to deploy her energy, or she was dangerous to be around.

January 20, 1988, Santa Anita Racetrack, California

At Santa Anita on January 20, 1988, the fillies loaded into their gates for the stakes event, and Winning Colors broke in scintillating style at the bell, quickly establishing a one-and-a-half length lead, blasting into the first left-hand turn. She started the long run down the backstretch, and Stevens tried to rate her energy, but she continued to pour on her early speed, again running sprinter-like quarter-mile and half-mile fractions of 22 seconds flat, and 45-and-four-fifths seconds.

Lukas was staring with concern at the track's tote board to see these early fraction times posted. He was not happy with what they saw for her first half-mile pace. What he saw was that she was not rating for her jockey!

Stevens was trying to get her to relax, trying to teach her through his hands on the reins, to reserve her extraordinary energy and speed. He was amazed the moment she seemed to understand what he was trying to teach her; the change was fast as she suddenly showed a new sensibility, and relaxed. For the first time in her racing career, she was obeying him, and not running off.

Winning Colors entered the second turn two lengths in front. Still she was cruising at such a high rate of speed that the other fillies were overmatched early. As she exited the final turn, she was four lengths in front! Stevens noted that she always seemed to run faster in the turns. For the first time that day, her jockey asked her to run by letting his reins out a notch and chirping to her, "Let's go girl…let's go girl… now…. Hah…. Hah…. Hah." She was happy to be set free and use her bundled power and energy as she jetted away from the field, winning easily, without ever being asked for her best, winning by six-and-a-half lengths over the other 3-year-old fillies.

Under his helmet, Stevens was smiling because she had just shown him the one thing he was hoping to see—that she was intelligent and was learning to be rated. She was not just a one-dimensional, speed crazy horse. The morning training sessions designed by Jeff Lukas, with Stevens riding her at dawn, were paying off. Champion racehorses are not just born, they are taught, coached, and developed. The Lukas team had patiently waited for this moment, and they now understood she was maturing into a potential champion racehorse. Winning Colors was showing the sense and intelligence to go with her natural brilliant athletic ability.

CHAPTER 2

Would You Bet Your Life on a 50-1 Shot?

January 23, 1988, Agua Caliente Racetrack, Tijuana, Mexico

It was dark in Mark "Miami" Paul's bedroom when the sound of the telephone jarred him awake.

"Miami, wake up! Today's the day. You need to take me to Mexico."

"It's Saturday. Dino, go back to sleep."

"No. Wake the hell up. I've been pouring over the numbers all the damn night long. She's going to win the Kentucky Derby...and we are going to cash a bet for a quarter million. For sure."

"I was at the Lakers game and I got into the Forum Club...until one a.m."

"Miami...man...wake up. If you don't take me...I'll go myself. I know her odds are going to drop if we don't bet her soon, and it will cost us tens of thousands of dollars when she wins the race."

"Dino, don't go alone to Tijuana. You know how oblivious you are when you're gambling. You'll get killed, man. Give me a second...."

Miami got up and stumbled into the bathroom, threw some water on his face, toweled off, and went back to the telephone. "OK... Let me get some coffee and wake up. I'll pick you up in an hour. Dino, you really think this filly can win the Derby?"

28

Miami took his time through a coffee and toast breakfast, showered, and went to his closet. He picked out a teal colored cotton t-shirt, and white linen slacks. He reviewed all 11 of his *Miami Vice* styled jackets, each with three-quarter length sleeves, in silk pastel colors. He grabbed a white one, and donned (without socks) one pair of his six sets of white tennis shoes. Now he could go pick up Dino Mateo in Santa Monica.

At 9:00 a.m., Dino got into Miami's red turbo 300Z sports car with the hardtop roof down, blaring Phil Collins on the stereo. The two men hit the 405 and headed south towards Mexico. Getting over the first 135 miles from Los Angeles to the Mexican border was the easy part and the two best friends were mostly quiet for over an hour.

As the bright Southern California sun rose and warmed the car through the open roof, they grew more awake and talkative. A gambler's blood pressure always soars on the way to an event. The prospect of winning or losing hundreds, or in the case of Miami and Dino, thousands of dollars that day was adrenalizing, at least for Miami. Going to a different country to get the action down heightened Miami's anticipation, but Dino appeared unfazed.

"Dino, do you know what the last three miles from border to the track have been called for over 70 years? The Road to Hell. Man, this is Tijuana. TJ! Be careful of these guys down here, Dino."

"It's the road to a huge score for us Miami...as long as they are still offering Winning Colors at odds of 50-1. I'm scared all right...scared they'll lower her odds, or they won't even take our bet on her to win the Derby."

"I tapped out on the Lakers last night."

"I watched. Great game! Kareem had 24...right? And they came from behind to win by one."

"Yeah...but they were favored by eight. They are the world champions, for God's sake. Against the Knicks...who suck...but last night they looked good. I hate Ewing."

"I told you, I bet the Lakers' futures again...to win back-to-back titles. I think they will. Do you have your money for the bet? I told you to save your money for this."

"Kind of," said Miami as his hands gripped the steering wheel. "I swear I am never making a bet that you don't make with me again. I suck at picking winners."

Four hours later, Miami parked on the US side of the border. The two friends walked across the International Bridge catwalk to enter Mexico. The crossing was swarming with both Americans and Mexicans, and as they always did in close quarter gambling environments, Dino and Miami put their wallets into the front pockets of their pants and kept their hands in front of their bodies to fend off pickpockets. Moments after they crossed into Mexico, taxi drivers besieged them and tried to herd them toward waiting cars. They chose a dark green taxi and told the driver, "Agua Caliente Racetrack."

Miami was sweating in the hot cab, even on a January day, but he was afraid to open his window, as he'd seen people in the middle of the street holding chickens and all kinds of crazy goods, with hundreds of vendor carts lining the roads, hoping to attract the tourists walking and driving by.

"Why in the hell are they selling us live chickens in the road?" Miami asked Dino. "Like what the hell would we do? Take a few live chickens home to our houses for dinner tonight? 'Hey honey, here's a few live chickens for you. Fry 'em up.'"

The vendors were selling everything from live iguanas to leather underwear. When the taxi stopped at a red light, vendors surrounded the car, swarming them while motioning them to roll down the windows and buy their wares. A young teenager climbed onto the hood of the taxi and started washing the front window before the taxi driver yelled an obscenity in Spanish at him, and he bolted away.

Miami looked at Dino who seemed at peace. Dino appeared blissful. Miami had seen this with Dino many times before, at California tracks like Santa Anita, Del Mar, and Hollywood Park, and in the Las Vegas mega hotels. Dino was in a hyper-focused gambling trance.

Both men were 30 years of age, but Dino was much shorter and heavier than Miami. He was wearing blue jeans, a blue golf shirt, and expensive New Balance running shoes. Miami doubted Dino had ever run a mile in his life. Dino always looked like he got dressed in a hurry. He could make an expensive suit look disheveled. Dino was a real estate appraiser for a commercial firm based in Los Angeles. He spent his mornings analyzing spread sheets and valuations, and afternoons pouring over horseracing data to uncover betting opportunities for his own bankroll.

As a commercial real estate broker, Miami worked early in the morning on the telephone with wealthy East Coast clients buying California income properties. This left him with free time in the California afternoons and on weekends. In early 1988, the average interest rate on a mortgage was 10.5 percent. The prime rate was 10 percent. Real estate deals were all dropping out because of the high interest rates. Miami was learning a new reality; gambling was fun when you didn't feel the sting of the losses or need the wins. He had always made money in real estate before, but he had zero deals in escrow now.

The smell of burning trash filled their nostrils as the cab got closer to Agua Caliente. Tijuana, on a Sunday morning, was brimming with business and Miami noticed that the children working alongside their parents wore mostly clean clothes despite the squalor alongside the road. When the cab hit a pothole, Miami's head bounced into the cab's low roof. He turned to Dino and said, "Man, you are incredible. You take me to a third world country to bet on a race still five months away. Where the hell did I find you?"

At the Tijuana racetrack the two friends could gamble on future sporting events like the Kentucky Derby, other big national thoroughbred races, and major sporting events, up to 11 months before the events were decided. Dino had done research and was excited to find that the Agua Caliente racetrack's future book gave much bigger odds than what could be gotten (legal or illegal) the day of the race or game from a Las Vegas bookmaker. The odds were much, much bigger. Often a horse that would wind up at 5-1 the day of race could be bet big at 50-1, 100-1, or even 300-1, many months before the actual race would be run. The Las Vegas casinos offered these same types of futures bets, at much more attractive betting venues, surrounded by swimming pools, sexy cocktail waitresses, craps and blackjack tables, but the Vegas odds were much less generous, and the Vegas casinos limited the amount of money they would accept in futures bets. It amazed the two gamblers that a multi-million-dollar Vegas casino would sometimes refuse a $1,000 future bet on a long shot Derby horse, but the casinos were shockingly conservative with their horse betting limits. Las Vegas was once the wild gambling frontier, but to Miami and Dino, Agua Caliente now offered far more opportunity for bold wagers from adventurous gamblers.

The owners of this Mexican racetrack were not being generous or stupid with the odds they offered. Just like the Las Vegas casinos, in futures betting, the house kept one huge advantage. If the horse did not run in the race, they kept all the money bet on that horse, with no refunds.

For the Kentucky Derby, the biggest race of the year, the bookmakers would post advance odds on over 300 horses to win the race. Horses would be listed that would have no chance to be in the race, yet alone win. Even to be invited into a race like the Kentucky Derby, the horse has to keep winning stakes races to be entered in the big race.

Miami and Dino had seen horses listed on the Mexican futures betting odds list that were already dead from illness or injury. Literally dead. In fairness to the Mexican track, extremely generous odds were offered.

The taxi dropped them off at the racetrack entrance at 1:30 p.m., but it was more like they had gone 60 years back in time. This racetrack had once been one of the grandest in the world but wasn't looking so impressive anymore. It had opened in 1929 at a staggering cost of $2,500,000 ($36,000,000 in 1988 valuation), just in time for the end of the Roaring Twenties and the Wall Street crash of 1929. The once elegant racetrack had gone bust many times since it opened, like in 1935, when the Mexican government declared all gambling illegal for a short time. The track always managed to recover. For decades, the track had been an opulent place for a mostly American clientele to drink, party, and gamble, with an excellent hotel, spa, and a casino.

The Agua Caliente track was Las Vegas before Las Vegas legalized casino gambling in 1931.

Now in 1988, it was out of place again with its huge fountains, soaring staircases, and grand archways, leading to cigar and cigarette smoke filled rooms, lined with gamblers who were watching dozens of television monitors beaming in races from US racetracks.

The local Agua Caliente Sunday live races were about to start. Miami located a table near the betting windows after he'd purchased a Mexican version of the *Daily Racing Form* and a cold beer. He could smell tacos and homemade tortillas at a vendor's stand. Young Mexican guards with old carbine rifles hanging from their necks from thick, brown leather straps were in each room. Guns and guards were everywhere.

Miami looked at Dino who was sitting across the table and said, "I don't know if we should be more afraid of the guards or the customers robbing us."

Over the last 15 years, Dino and Miami had spent most of their days off at racetracks from California to Florida. The private turf clubs at Hollywood Park and Santa Anita, which required a coat and tie for admittance, were their usual hangouts. Those posh, high society Los Angeles clubs with a maître 'd and reservations required to get a table were nothing like this betting joint.

Miami looked to his left to see a table of horse gamblers dressed in cheap, colorful shirts that might have fit their fat bodies 30 years earlier, but now made them look like ugly American tourists. Two of them had colorful red and yellow shorts on, with black dress socks and black scuffed up dress shoes. The horse gamblers at the tables surrounding him were getting louder as the cocktail waitress brought them more and more trays of huge green margaritas covered with salt around the glass edges. They seemed more interested in getting drunk and partying than seriously betting the horses.

Four women were sitting at two tables in the back of the race book; all were flirting with the margarita-drinking men who surrounded them. The women were aged 35 to 45 and were not unattractive from a distance, but seen from up close, they had on way too much heavy make-up for a Sunday. They didn't look like they'd just come from church in their low cut, colorful, short dresses, and three-inch high heels.

"Who do you like in the first race, gringo?" Miami asked Dino.

Dino always spoke fast...very fast. "I couldn't care less about a cheap group of broken-down Mexican horses in a $1,800 claiming race."

Miami watched Dino keep his focus, thinking about the future running of the Kentucky Derby. Dino was staring, transfixed, at the betting windows.

It takes a special kind of gambler not to get distracted by the action, noise, and excitement of all the betting opportunities around him. Las Vegas is full of stories of guys dropping $2,000 at the blackjack table because they were just trying to walk over to the $7.95 buffet table.

Dino pushed his chair back, walked up to a betting window, and asked the Mexican ticket seller to confirm the exact current future book odds for the Kentucky Derby, the Super Bowl, and the NBA World Championship. He was at the window for nearly 10 minutes asking about the odds on certain teams and several horses, and a long line of anxious horse bettors was growing angry behind him, getting more and more pissed as they worried about being shut out from making their wagers on the first live Tijuana horserace.

A swarthy American gambler behind Dino heard what odds he was asking about, and shouted, "Asshole! The NBA Championship is in six goddamn months. Let me bet on this fucking TJ race that's going off in three minutes!"

"Find another window," Dino shouted back at him.

Miami saw the reaction, and it wasn't good. The guy looked drunk and glassy eyed. He grabbed Dino's shoulder and spun him around hard.

Miami moved in fast. At six-foot-three, 210 pounds, blond and blue eyed, he stood out at the Mexican track, and now towered over Dino and the short drunken gambler. Miami put his hand on the shoulders of the two men. "Whoa, guys…let's have some fun and win some money… let's settle down. Hey, amigo, go make your bet…no problems here." Miami stared down into the drunk gambler's eyes.

Then Miami took Dino by the arm and led him back to his table. "Dino, let's not get killed here…OK? I need you alive. Why are you always getting into trouble?"

Dino was oblivious to the party and other gamblers around them. The unique thing about Dino was that he was a proven winner in a game of constant losers. Other gamblers wanted the action, the lifestyle, and the girls, but all Dino wanted was to win money. Miami would start having cocktails early in the day, but Dino would stay up until four a.m. drinking coffee while studying past race performances or team statistics, getting ready to make a well-planned strategic wager. Miami learned to stay with Dino and keep him out of trouble; if he were focused on a bet, Dino wouldn't notice an incoming mortar attack.

Several times, Miami missed out on huge money-making payoffs because Dino had made a bet while Miami was courting women, enjoying cocktails, or working out in the gym. Miami had learned to keep Dino in his sights at the Las Vegas race books, or at the track, because when Dino hit the betting windows, Miami wanted always to be a part of that. Miami made far more money than Dino in his day job, but Dino was the bigger gambler for sure. Dino bet big money on the daily horseraces, future book sporting events like the Super Bowl or NBA playoffs, and select NFL football games. Dino could tell you exactly the type of offensive or defensive game statistics it took to win a Super Bowl, and what the strength of schedule was for every NFL playoff contender. Dino was cheap with his money, until he saw a betting opportunity, then he would bet with both hands and no fear.

For example, during the past summer, in 117-degree heat at the Flamingo Hotel in Las Vegas, Miami and Dino were at a three-day horse betting contest. They had been losing money consistently for two and a half days and finally Miami had gotten tired and disgusted of repeatedly losing bets. He went to the craps table to take a break. Miami left Dino alone for thirty minutes, and when he came back, Dino was standing at the cashier's window collecting $4,800 in cash from a 23-1 shot he keyed in the exacta in the final Santa Anita race of the day.

Never again was Miami going to let that happen and now he stayed with Dino like a big protective guard dog for his smaller friend.

Professional horse gamblers typically purchase the past performances newspaper published by the *Daily Racing Form*. They'll study for hours to handicap a horse's past performances, hoping to find a winning bet opportunity. Dino would study the horses' past performances, the trainers' records, and even the horse owner's patterns.

When Dino and Miami started going to the track together, they were only 16 years old. Young Dino noticed that owners who looked like they were cast from the Mafia movie *The Godfather* would often win races. So, Dino started betting on horses whose owners and trainers last names ended in a vowel. If there was a Corleone, a Gino, or a Vito in the name, Dino was hammering him at the windows, and they won more than their share, often at big odds. One day, Dino picked a winning horse that paid 22-1 because the owner's last name was Romano. That tip turned $200 into $4,600 for Miami and Dino.

The hardest part back then for Miami and Dino was just getting into the track, as at only 16 they were underage, but still they found ways to get in to gamble. After school, the boys would wait at the front gate and give a degenerate looking gambler a free betting ticket if he would let them accompany him through the front admissions gate. They learned to wear suits and ties to the track to look older, and carried men's briefcases with them, trying to look like distinguished young businessmen. It usually worked at the tracks because what 16-year-old kids could possibly be betting at the $50 and $100 large wagers windows? It was also true that they'd be thrown out on a regular basis for being underage. When it happened, they changed hats as a disguise and came back through another entrance.

Now adults in Tijuana at Agua Caliente, an attractive cocktail waitress with shiny, thick black hair tied in a red bow, wearing a short black skirt and red heels, came over to their table to deliver the bucket of beers on ice Miami had ordered. She smiled directly at Miami, and then asked them both, "What are your names?"

Miami glanced at her nametag and said, "Dino...meet Camila. Camila, meet Dino. I'm Miami. Camila, Dino is a big gambler and is here to make all our dreams come true. You should join him. If all goes well today at the track, you will never have to work again."

Camila seemed to be grasping about 10 percent of what Miami was saying and smiled while asking Dino if he wanted her to open a beer for him. Dino declined and ordered a Coke as she left.

"I'm starting to like it here," said Miami. "Dino can you not get into another fight at the betting window, because I want to live."

Dino looked at the full bucket of beers on ice and said, "Miami, you have to drive us home!"

"If you keep arguing with the customers we won't have to worry about the drive, because we'll be stabbed to death long before my driving is an issue."

"How much money do you have on you?"

"Enough for the beers and…I don't know about the Winning Colors bet."

"Miami, the odds are incredible here…way better than Vegas. We need to start coming here every month."

Another thing about Dino that was different than any other gambler Miami had met was Dino's specialty with long shots. Where most big bettors would bet $5,000 on a football game at basically even money odds, Dino would bet $5,000 or $10,000 on a team to win the Super Bowl at 6-1, 10-1, 20-1 or more. Sure, he lost far more bets than he won every year, but when he cashed, he really cashed for big money. Same thing on horses, as Dino would bet only on long-shot horses offered at 6-1 odds or higher. If he lost five in a row and then won one race, he was going home with a big profit.

Now he was on to another big opportunity. "Our horse Winning Colors, she is still 50-1, that's incredible. When she wins…our $5,000 bet will pay out $250,000. I have my $2,500," said Dino.

"You are serious about this, aren't you? I need to keep a few bucks on the side for beers, margaritas, and dinner. I know you told me to save up for this bet…but man, I've got nothing working! Nothing." Miami shook his head. "My office deal in escrow cancelled Friday. I really should just keep this money for my car payment, pay bills, and maybe just take Ava out to dinner."

"I get it…things are tight…but this is different. Even if you don't bet another race this year…you gotta make this bet!"

"If you say so. Dino…I believe in you, man…here's $2,500 for your horse." Miami handed Dino a white envelope under the table. "I don't think we should make the bet until right before we leave. I don't want these assholes to see we have real money with us. I think they would kill us for 20 bucks."

"No way! Let's bet her now before the odds go down! This is the bet of a lifetime."

"Holy shit, Dino, you have never said that before…ever. You're usually quiet about your betting opinions."

Now Miami knew Dino was there to make a serious wager. He believed one of the richest horse owners in the world might enter his female horse in the 1988 Kentucky Derby. A billionaire so rich he had owned an NFL team. Dino knew the former NFL owner's horse could win the Derby. Dino believed this horse would win the Derby. Traditionally only male horses, colts, enter the Kentucky Derby, and in 113 years, only two female horses had ever won the race. Dino thought that was about to change with a filly named Winning Colors.

Dino was a slow walker and could never keep up with his tall friend—outside of a gambling venue, that is. When they got within 500 yards of a betting facility, suddenly Dino could move like a racehorse on methamphetamines. Dino would then suddenly be walking so fast Miami would struggle to stay in sight of him. Dino had perfected a form of gambling radar that allowed him to dart in and out of pedestrians in order not to get shut out of a bet. Now on the betting floor of Agua Caliente, Dino's senses were fully alive, and he knew that the betting decisions he was about to make could change his life.

Dino didn't wait. He jumped up and dashed to the betting window like a 350-yard quarter horse at Los Alamitos racetrack. Miami thought, Damn I've got to see this, and came up on Dino's right side, at the betting window.

Miami listened as Dino told the ticket writer, "Five thousand US dollars on the Kentucky Derby future book. Winning Colors at 50-1, to win $250,000 on the race."

The ticket writer's eyebrows raised, and he became agitated. "Jefe ven aca! Mas dinero en Winning Colors," he shouted to his supervisor.

An older man with a gold tooth and an expensive looking shirt came into view. He spoke in Spanish with the ticket writer; the men went back and forth, and then he said to them, under his breath in English, "Another bet on this stupid bitch of a horse? Un momento por favor." The supervisor then walked to a back room, out of sight.

Now Dino looked worried. Miami asked, "What's up, Dino?"

"I think someone else already made a huge bet on her to win the Derby. Probably way bigger than our bet. That's what I have been afraid of and why I woke you up so early today. With our bet they can lose another $250,000 if she wins. It's too big a bet for him to accept himself. Too much risk to the track. He needs approval. Man, I hope they take this bet. Miami, if they do they are idiots because 50-1 on her is a gift."

"Someone's an idiot here," Miami responded, "and I hope it's not us."

The supervisor came back out to the window with a good looking, much younger man with dark wavy hair, much like an Elvis impersonator. The new man was dressed in a crisp white shirt and groomed perfectly in the way only handsome Latin guys can look. "Señors…a girl horse cannot beat the boys in the Kentucky Derby, my friends. Are you sure? Save your money, amigos."

Dino didn't hesitate and said, "I know we are crazy…but still we would like to make that bet, and please make it into three or four separate smaller, different tickets, thank you."

The young Mexican boss waited a long time, thinking before speaking. Then he smiled with his perfect white teeth and said to the ticket writer, "Take their money. A filly will not win the Kentucky Derby."

CHAPTER 3

Cartel Trouble

Racetracks breed more rumors than horses. The bettors are afraid of secret information known only to the insiders on fast horses that they fear will beat their personal selections. Every track's grooms, bartenders, and valet parking attendants have a hot tip that only they seem to be privy to. Track regulars call these "steam horses," and some will bet double or triple their normal amount on questionable information, often given from a blue-collar worker.

Miami had once seen one of the best handicappers in the country, the famous "Professor" Gordon Jones, drop his own best bet of the day because some Las Vegas based guy called him on his cell phone with a supposed steam horse. This steam horse ran last in the race.

Dino, who toiled for hours each night viewing the horses' past performances to find betting opportunities, wondered why anyone would trust a bartender or a car park attendant to get betting information. He always asked the information suppliers the same question, "What kind of car do you drive?" Dino figured if inside information was working so well for him he should have a new high-end model parked out front.

Miami and Dino were hearing rumors about other track regular bettors that had also made futures Derby bets on Winning Colors in Las Vegas and even at the Mexican track. The best source for track betting information was a man named Twenty Percent Tim who had a good gig working at Santa Anita and the other tracks in Southern California.

When a winning track ticket exceeds odds of 300-1, the Internal Revenue Service (IRS) is suddenly a partner to the bettor on a winning ticket. That winning ticket requires cashiers to ask for the gambler's social security number and other form of identification before cashing out a large payout. The IRS keeps 20 percent withholding of the proceeds, and the gambler must report this income on a tax return. The gambler can deduct documented betting losses against betting income, but few horseplayers bother to do the paperwork.

Twenty Percent Tim would stand around the cashiers' windows after a long shot won a race, asking gamblers if they had a "signer," meaning a ticket they had to sign for with an IRS form. If the gambler did have a signer ticket, Twenty Percent Tim would peel off hundreds or thousands of dollars out of pockets stuffed with greenbacks and pay cash on the spot for that gambler's winning ticket—less 20 percent, of course. Bettors often don't want to give out their personal information and seldom have their social security card for identification on them.

People who had so little income that they paid no taxes were friends of Twenty Percent Tim's. He would get them to cash the winning betting tickets and give him back the tax refund. Dino had noticed that Twenty Percent Tim did drive a new Mercedes and wore an expensive suit to the track every day. Other than the practice was illegal, Twenty Percent Tim had a successful and thriving business on his hands.

After a day at Santa Anita, Dino, Miami, and Twenty Percent Tim were sitting in a bar near the track enjoying happy hour. Dino asked Twenty Percent Tim about Mexican futures betting at Agua Caliente racetrack, and he responded, "Great odds…if you get paid."

"What the hell are you talking about? I heard the owner of the track is one of the richest men in Mexico."

"First, that racetrack is in trouble and will go out of business soon. They have no horses there anymore because everyone is now satellite simulcasting races into their own local track, and they don't have to cross the damn border to get some action down. Second, the Mexico track's owner better be very damn rich. I know they already took one bet for $20,000 at 50-1 on your filly to win the Derby, and dozens of other bets like yours."

Miami and Dino jumped out of their chairs to stand up next to Twenty Percent Tim. "Don't fuck with us, Twenty Percent," Miami told him while getting within inches of his face. "Who would bet $20,000 on her?" He looked Tim straight in the eye and told him, "I need to know who the big player is."

"I would, but never in Mexico. Shit, they'll kill you down there for 100 bucks. I know the guy that made the 20K bet and he thinks he is going to win $1,000,000 if your horse hits. I hear the owner of the racetrack is a cartel guy, too. I say no way they'll pay this sucker. They'll never find his body!"

Miami looked at Twenty Percent.

"You know I can't tell you."

"OK, don't tell me, just direct me. I'm sure I know him already."

"You do, for sure…think about who has had a big score recently."

"Bernie…Big Bernie," said Dino. "He hit a big Pick 6 at Hollywood Park in November, for $200,000 plus. I bet it's him. He's a big player and has the cash."

Twenty Percent Tim was quiet but looked Dino right in the eye, held his gaze for five seconds, then nodded his head up and down before turning and walking away. Miami waited a few seconds, looked at Dino, and said, "Let me talk to him privately. Alone. Big Bernie is always asking me to take him out to the clubs after the races. He's like 350 pounds now I would guess, maybe more. He wants me to introduce him to girls, but he thinks getting dressed up is putting on a new bowling shirt. I'll have to take him out and get some booze into him."

Dino sat down and was quiet. He was convinced that Winning Colors was the best horse in the likely Derby field. "I honestly wouldn't change my selection for any other horse in the race," he said to Miami.

"Well, she probably won't win anyway."

"Don't say that! You're wrong! She is maybe the best bet I have ever made in my whole lifetime of analyzing and betting horses, sports, real estate, anything, and I was actually going to tell you we should go back to Mexico and bet more on her after her next race!"

"Oh, great fucking idea, we can become bigger targets than we are already. I'll take out a bigger second mortgage tomorrow and really get down on her. By the way Dino, do you know a life insurance agent?"

The next day the two friends started to research Agua Caliente racetrack and the track's owner, Jorge Hank Rhon They didn't know where to start and were hampered by inability to speak or read Spanish. Dino figured a library was the best place to start. He told Miami he would meet him at the one in Beverly Hills at 3:00 p.m.

"What's a library?" Miami responded.

"It's a place where they keep books. Remember when you went to college?"

"Not really. Can we get a drink there?"

"I think we should look for magazine and newspaper articles on the racetrack and its owner. They should have them there on microfiche."

"I know how to fish. You get an ice chest full of beer and...."

"Seriously, we need to find out who the hell we are dealing with. Who are these guys?"

At the library, the friends asked for help from an older librarian. She pointed toward a dark haired, younger woman wearing a print dress with a bow at the neckline and low white heels. Her nametag read Amalia Duran. She spoke to them in English but with an unmistakable Spanish accent. Amalia was perhaps 32, had olive skin, wore glasses, and was quite cute, in a reserved way. Dino took immediate interest in her and explained that they were considering doing business with the Agua Caliente racetrack and its owner, Jorge Rhon.

"Amalia, have you ever been to a racetrack?" asked Dino.

"No, but it sounds fun."

"It's a wonderful, beautiful, special place. We...I...will take you there. The racehorses are beautiful, and it's a fun place for a date. I mean more like a lunch...if you are interested?"

"I would love to see the horses. Is it safe for them to race?"

"It's only dangerous for the gamblers like Dino and me," said Miami. She tilted her head toward Dino. "You're a gambler?"

"Sometimes. But I really go because it's the most amazing sport in the entire world. It's called 'the sport of kings.' You'll see. The horses are beautiful, and the baby 2-year-old colts and fillies are making their first starts this time of year. You can feed them carrots when we go, Amalia."

43

Dino stared at Miami while biting his upper lip and discreetly giving him a two-handed, palms down sign with both hands to be quiet.

Miami smiled and asked, "Is there a bar here?" then walked away to leave the two of them alone.

The research became much more enjoyable for Dino over the coming weeks as he and Amalia dated. He took her to a play and a comedy club. She was quiet but liked to laugh when Dino told her something funny.

Amalia helped Dino and Miami investigate information on Agua Caliente and the track's owner. Dino got Amalia to go to the Los Angeles library's downtown branch that had more microfiche and access to the Tijuana papers and magazines. She was bilingual and learned that Rhon's father, the former mayor of Mexico City, had become one of the richest men in Mexico and had been quoted as saying, "A politician who is poor, is a poor politician." In 1984, the father gifted his son, Jorge Hank Rhon, the Agua Caliente horse and dog racetrack. Later, Amalia found articles in the library on the younger Rhon that portrayed him as a saint, but also linked him to drug dealing and massive political corruption.

Jorge Rhon was the same age as Miami and Dino—31. He was a colorful character who often sported a red crocodile skin vest, and owned Mexico's Grupo Caliente, which included a chain of off-track horse betting locations, a dog racing track, a hotel, a huge shopping mall in Tijuana, and his Agua Caliente racetrack. Grupo Caliente had for some time been trying to get sports betting on Mexican events, as well as US events, legalized in Mexico, but had so far been unsuccessful. Rhon ran the Miss Mexico beauty pageant and had just hosted the World Boxing title fight between Julio César Chávez and Danilo Cabrera. His house looked down on the Mexican track and was known as one of the largest mansions in Tijuana. The house had a private zoo with a collection of 20,000 wild animals, including monkeys, bears, camels, elephants, big cats, pygmy hippos, and a variety of birds, snakes, and wolves.

"This is all good. He's rich!" Miami shouted.

"Apparently, personally owning wild and dangerous animals is common among wealthy cartel leaders," Amalia said as she showed the gamblers an article to confirm the information.

The big cats always fascinated Rhon and he drove around with a baby white tiger in his Mercedes until he was caught by the US Border Patrol and fined $25,000. His personal cheetah once escaped and was hit by a pick-up truck near the track. Stories surfaced that for weeks he didn't feed his Bengal tigers. Then he released other live animals into the cat's cages for entertainment, and he and his friends watched the tigers devour horses, burros, and goats, in a violent blood bath.

"This guy is a cartel guy!" said Dino.

Amalia went on translating the research and telling them Rhon was nicknamed, "Tigre Blanco," or, in English, "White Tiger." He loved to throw wild parties featuring bullfights and cockfights on his massive estate. Gambling and drinking were the order of the day.

Almost weekly, scandalous articles about Rhon and Agua Caliente were written in the extremely popular local Tijuana newspaper, *Zeta*. The famous (and prolific) reporter, Hector Felix Miranda, known by his pen name, El Gato, penned a column titled "Un Poco de Algo," or, "A Little Something."

The articles about Rhon were plentiful, with El Gato often implying that Rhon was a drug sniffing, womanizing, rich boy who was running the racetrack toward ruin, but he was also a philanthropist and generous to the poor. El Gato often mentioned Rhon's business associates. Amalia said some of these associates were possibly on the United States Drug Enforcement Administration's (DEA) wanted lists, with the DEA offering rewards of tens of thousands of dollars to anyone who helped capture the brutal and dangerous drug traffickers.

El Gato infuriated Rhon when he chronicled Rhon's infidelities and girlfriends. The reporter was apparently socially friendly with Rhon at times and attended many of his parties but wrote of Rhon's cocaine use at the decadent parties, an accusation Rhon always denied.

There were written allegations of fixed horseraces and fraudulent bets. The relationship between the reporter and Rhon seemed acrimonious. In a March 1988 article, El Gato was invited to a beauty pageant held at Agua Caliente and the journalist wrote, "I have seven lives like cats, but I do not know how many I have left." El Gato seemed to be implying that he was afraid of Rhon.

Since 1985 new off-track "simulcasting" betting facilities were opening throughout California, causing financial ruin for the Agua Caliente track in Tijuana. Gamblers could now stay in Southern California instead of crossing the border to bet. New technologies were changing the horse betting game and there were winners and losers at the bookmakers' level. The winners were the big US racetracks and the new US simulcasting facilities. The losers were the small tracks everywhere as bettors could now bet on the racing signals beamed in from the big classy tracks like Santa Anita, Hollywood Park, Churchill Downs, and Saratoga. Non-US, off-track betting facilities, and private illegal bookmakers, were left out in the cold.

Business was so bad at Agua Caliente that Rhon sold off his black, twin-engine Lockheed JetStar executive jet, as well as six of his beloved sports cars including a Ferrari. Rhon admitted the track was bleeding money. He declined to say how much money he has lost in horseracing since he was given the track in August 1985, but he did admit, "Let's just say that it totals in the millions. We have stables for over 1,000 horses and used to house between 800 and 1,000 horses every year. In the past year, we've only had between 150 and 280 horses."

Dino said, "Agua Caliente doesn't have enough horses and is dying. I bet that racetrack is bankrupt within a year now, because everyday horse bettors can just simulcast their bets in Del Mar. Why the hell would anyone go there now?"

Amalia had read rumors that the track company allowed Rhon to launder drug money, but there had never been any charges filed against Rhon; at least none that she could find. Rhon's nightclub, Iguana, and his restaurants in Tijuana, allegedly were favorites of the Arellano-Felix drug cartel. To reporters and sources in Tijuana, Rhon was viewed as "the richest man and most powerful" person in the infamous border town.

"Guys," said Amalia, "you are not going to believe this, but I've read in several articles that Rhon mixes the penises of tigers, lions, and dogs into his tequila and drinks it!"

"Really? Who does that?" Miami asked. "I'm sure that kind of guy won't mind paying off millions of dollars to us gringo horseplayers."

"Well at least he could probably afford to pay us," said Dino.

"Wouldn't it just be cheaper to have us killed?" asked Miami.

Later that night, Miami read up on Agua Caliente. Amalia had given him another article about how back in the 1960s, the racetrack did not pay the famous restaurant owner Earl Jones, owner of the Earl's Hamburger chain, $10,000 when he hit the 5-10 (the Mexican track's version of the Pick 6). They claimed it was because of a corrupt ticket writer, not the track refusing to pay.

Miami also read of a big 5-10 payout of $350,204 to one winning ticket 10 years earlier to a gambler. That night Miami didn't sleep well thinking about the track's apparent connection to the drug trade and its financial condition. He went to sleep thinking that maybe the 25-1 odds on Winning Colors in the Las Vegas future book would have been a better bet than 50-1 in Tijuana. He also knew that Dino just didn't think that way. Dino's life was about getting the edge in odds, and he knew his best friend would not have taken half the odds offered on the same horse in Mexico despite the risks. Hell, Miami thought, Dino would go to the African Congo if they had higher odds offered.

The next day, Dino checked on the current Las Vegas future betting odds on Winning Colors and learned she was now bet down to 12-1 in the Nevada casinos. He remained convinced she was a great bet and eagerly awaited her next start on a weekend in late February. Dino was now handicapping Winning Colors' next race and was wondering what Lukas would do next. Would he stay with conventional training methods and keep the star filly running against her own sex or become aggressive and go against the tougher male runners? He knew Lukas and Klein would have to decide soon.

The Derby was becoming a personal thorn to Lukas who could not win the biggest race despite having sent out more Derby entrants than any other trainer in history. The previous year he had won over $17,000,000 in purses and 22 Grade 1 races, but his lone Derby entrant ran fifth. Would he risk the humiliation and risk running a filly again? Or, would he keep the big gray Amazon running against her own sex and earn easier Grade 1 purses against the smaller fillies?

February 19, 1988, Santa Anita Racetrack, California

Fridays were always track days for Miami and Dino and they were wearing the required sports coats and ties while having lunch at the Santa Anita Turf Club restaurant. It was the perfect venue overlooking the track, and in the distance, snow-capped mountains to the north were visible. Miami was in a state of complete and total happiness watching the horses prance to the gate for the first race of the day. He enjoyed the sight of the jockeys' colorful silks as much as he enjoyed a glass of crisp California chardonnay. He ripped open the *Daily Racing Form's* past performances to see prospects for the race Winning Colors would run the next day. The Saturday race was a prestigious Grade 1 level stakes race. The level of horses that compete in stakes races are ranked in order: Overnight, Listed, Grade 3, Grade 2, and Grade 1. Approximately 100 elite Grade 1 stakes races are run each year in America. The Kentucky Derby, Preakness, Belmont, and Breeders' Cup races are all Grade 1, and are often referred to as the year's classic races.

Upon glancing at the competitors' track records, Miami saw a new immediate threat to Winning Colors. "Jesus Christ, Dino," he said, "have you looked at this New York filly named Goodbye Halo? They flew her in to compete with Winning Colors tomorrow. Shit! This filly keeps destroying her fields. She won her first race by eight lengths, and then won the Demoiselle Stakes at Aqueduct by 10 lengths! That's a Grade 1 stakes in New York! That damn horse can really run."

"I saw her last race in the Starlet Stakes. I don't think she can handle Winning Colors. Our girl has too much early speed and Goodbye Halo will be too far back to catch her."

"Goodbye Halo won that race by three-and-a-half lengths and it's a Grade 1, too. I'm nervous as hell for tomorrow."

"I'm hammering Winning Colors tomorrow at the windows. You'll see," said Dino.

CHAPTER 4

Stakes Class

Miami was a top sales broker in his office. He was used to making money and this new reality—lack of income—was causing him to doubt his career choice. On October 19, 1987, the historic financial event known as Black Monday had happened. On that day, the DOW dropped from 2,400 to 1,500 in a day. Four months later, investors still had no confidence to pull the trigger on any real estate deal, especially with the insane interest rates. Something has to give, or I am going to have to take a J.O.B., and stop going to the track, he thought.

Miami was not sleeping well. He had another problem—a $45,000 second mortgage coming due in less than two months on his two-bedroom condo in Westwood, and he didn't have the money, or now, even prospects to get the money. He tried to get the loan refinanced through a bank but had been turned down due to lack of equity in his unit.

The current lender had called Miami the week before asking what his plan was to pay off the maturing loan.

"I'm planning on winning a large bet on a horse race," Miami said, and then added, "just kidding...don't worry...I've got it covered."

Besides the mortgage, Miami had even more on his mind. He'd had another date that night with Ava Bouchon. She was smart, tall, classy, exotic, and dressed with great style and taste. Ava had a top marketing executive position in downtown Los Angeles, and a big corner office, but Miami was convinced she spent 150 percent of her income on clothes. Based on her wardrobe, he figured she was probably making more money than he was in his commercial real estate (commission only) business. She was flying all over the world because of her work and appeared to be killing it. Whatever she was doing, she had his attention. She was fun to be with, but he wasn't sure what she thought of him.

Miami first met Ava while they were both on vacation in the mountains over the Christmas holidays, when there was no racing. They had been having some fun together on several dates, but now Miami was thinking that having a steady girlfriend could be cool. She seemed interested, but he couldn't really tell. She was keeping her feelings guarded. Being with someone that could understand the passion he had for thoroughbred horse racing was uncommon. He was happily confused.

He was so confused that he was planning to break one of his most important and strictest codes in life: Never bring a woman along when gambling.

He made it through the next workday on Friday and that night he picked up Ava with the convertible top down and took her to a restaurant in Malibu. Ava looked great, but she kept asking about what hat to wear at Santa Anita tomorrow.

Miami didn't tell her all the details, but women's hats at the racetrack were a total annoyance to him. On big days at the track, when the best horses in racing and the best gambling opportunities of the racing year were present, it seemed that women only wanted to look at, talk about, and be seen in huge, over-stuffed hats. Sometimes on big race days, Miami couldn't see over the women's hats to watch the race, as they had entire fruit baskets perched on top of their heads.

"Ava, promise me you won't wear a hat to the track."

"I already picked it out. You'll love it. It's small and delicate."

"You're kidding…those track hats are ugly."

"You expect me to take fashion advice from a guy that has 11 identical jackets from a character on a TV show?"

"They're not identical… I have three different colors."

Miami had given the waiter his credit card, but it was declined.

"Let me get this," she volunteered.

"No, I've got it, Ava." He put down another card that he hoped had a positive balance on it. It went through.

50

It was quiet on the drive back down Pacific Coast Highway toward Westwood, until Miami opened up to Ava. "Right now, being a commercial real estate broker is nearly impossible," he said. "I'm struggling to get deals closed."

"You don't have to explain. Interest rates are high. I know."

"Not just high, they are over 10 percent...everyone's scared. The stock market is a mess, too."

"I'm sorry. It has to be difficult." She smiled at him and put her hand to his face. "Thanks for sharing with me."

"I've always been successful...and I will be again."

February 20, 1988, Santa Anita Racetrack, California

The next morning, Miami brought Ava coffee and opened the curtains. The winter morning sun reflected off the Westwood skyline office towers. "My track buddy Dino is going to join us today. He's the best horse handicapper in the country. We're going to drive there with him because my car doesn't seat three."

"He's coming with us on our track date?"

"I never go to the track without him. If you want to win, believe me you always want him with us."

They relaxed as Ava made avocado and bacon omelets. She read the *Los Angeles Times* and *Hollywood Reporter* as Miami read the racing form, with the Saturday college basketball games on in the background, with the sound on mute. He was relaxed and had no interest in betting on the games today.

Later that morning they dressed for their afternoon at the turf club. Miami put on a teal blue sports jacket, crisp white dress shirt, and tied a blue silk tie as he told Ava for the first time about their recent bet on Winning Colors to win the Kentucky Derby, still three months away. He told her about how spectacular Winning Colors was, and that today she would have to defeat the best fillies in California to continue her advance toward the Derby and have a chance to beat the males.

"We've had five dates, and I've never seen you so excited to go anywhere as you seem today," she said. Ava smiled at him. She even seemed happy to accept that Dino was now going with them on this date.

"You'll see, Ava, it's so beautiful at Santa Anita. You'll love the mountains, and I'll get you right up close to the horses in the saddling paddock. The horses are gorgeous, and it'll be exciting. What will you do with all the money you'll win today? Oh, and bring some shoes that you can walk in the mud and dirt…and other horse stuff…in."

"Are you sure Winning Colors will win today?"

"She's undefeated, and Dino thinks she is the best 3-year-old in the country, even better than the male colts, and believe me, he knows what he is doing. He has made me a ton of money."

"I can't wait. It sounds fun!" Ava laughed harder than he'd ever heard her laugh as she disappeared into the closet. "Oh yeah…let me show you my hat." She came back out wearing one of the widest hats he had ever seen, with blue feathers jutting out on top, over her long auburn hair. "See… I told you it would be understated."

"Ava…it won't fit in the car."

"You just pick us some winners…and leave the fashion to me."

It wasn't just the hat. Miami was apprehensive. He had seen, time and time again, that the instant a gambler fell in love and started spending time with a woman, he would inevitably always go on the largest losing streak of his life. Lucky at love, unlucky at gambling was a common saying. However, unlucky at gambling did not necessarily lead to being lucky at love.

The February afternoon was a typical bright California winter day with temperatures in the mid-70s. Dino picked them up in his yellow, four-door Impala, blasting "Faith," by George Michael. Ava and Miami hopped in the back seat. Forty-five minutes later they arrived to find the track packed with fans, with long lines for the public to get through the turnstiles.

They ordered lunch at their usual turf club table overlooking the Santa Anita stretch. It was fun for Miami and Dino to have Ava at their table, and many of their usual gambling buddies stopped by to say hello and meet her.

"How often do you and Dino go to the track?" she asked.

Miami shrugged off the question.

"No really…how often do you and Dino go to the track?"

"We don't go to the track as much as we used too. Now we only go when it's open."

"Mark…so why does everyone here call you 'Miami?'"

"It's my nickname. No idea how it started…."

"I'll stick with Mark."

"I hope you do." He looked into her eyes and smiled.

When Ava stepped away, Dino told him, "She seems to really make you happy."

"She does. Just something about her is special. She's kind of like Winning Colors… tall…athletic…and very feisty, too."

The boys were not hitting any winners at all; their horses were not running well. Miami had been buying small denomination betting tickets for Ava all day. The races are exciting when your horses are competitive and involved in photo finish stretch runs, but today their betting selections were not in the outcomes of any of the races at the finish.

"Zip. Zero. Zilch. We have not cashed a single damn ticket today. Ava, I usually perform better than this."

"No, he doesn't," said Dino.

"Let me pick one…I'd like to win at least one race today. I need a winner!" said Ava.

"Sure…but, it's complicated. Dino can explain and help you understand the important stuff, like early speed, track post position bias, class, and closing internal fractions."

"Nah…I'm good…I like Quacky Ducky in the next race," she said as she smiled at Mark.

"Quacky Ducky? You're kidding, right?"

"It's a great name."

"Quacky Ducky it is." Miami went down to bet $20 to win for Ava on her horse and put $100 each for Dino and himself on Dino's race selection of Dancing Papa.

Dancing Papa went to an early lead and as he turned for home, he looked like a winner. A wall of closing horses charged late in a three-horse photo finish. Miami could tell Dancing Papa had faded and was not paying attention when the photo finish result was posted showing a

48-1 long shot: Ava's horse was the winner. Quacky Ducky had won for only the second time in twenty-three career starts, while Dancing Papa faded to third.

"How much did we win?" screamed Ava while proudly holding her winning ticket in the air.

"Uh. You won $960. Dino and I...we...we lost again...."

"Why didn't you bet on Quacky Ducky?"

"It's all good," Dino told Ava.

"I'm going to go cash my ticket...just point the way to the cashier's window...do you guys remember where it is?" She smiled as she left the table.

"She is a great girl, Miami, and I just don't believe in the women are bad luck at the track thing. In any given race, sure luck matters." Dino believed in his statistics, research, and hard work. Winning at the track was a formula to be deciphered, and, over a long period of time, he believed he would prevail. "And apparently she is a much better handicapper than you are. Picking Quacky Ducky at 48-1 was a mean piece of work."

"I told you she is special. Let's see who she likes in the ninth, after the Winning Colors race next up."

When Ava came back, Dino explained, "The race we came here for is coming next in 30 minutes. The absolute best stakes class fillies in the entire country are entered today against our girl Winning Colors. Goodbye Halo is the top East Coast champion, going against our West Coast champion filly Winning Colors. If she wins...when she wins... it will be a great day. No worries."

The Lukas stable was revolutionizing thoroughbred racing. Its horses were winning so many races that everyone they entered would be bet down to low odds. With so many high-class horses stabled in each Lukas barn across the nation, they often would have multiple horses running in the same race. The toughest race day competition for a Lukas horse was often another Lukas trained horse. The Lukas barn had become the leading stable in money won each year by running an elite string of horses simultaneously in Southern California, Kentucky, New York, and Florida. This was unheard of in the old school racing industry.

Lukas had now purchased his own private jet to scour the horse auctions and meet with affluent owners from Malibu to Manhattan. The other trainers resented this handsome Hollywood trainer, his jet, his Rolls Royce, and his attire. They disparaged him behind his back about his training techniques, the ones he'd learned in his quarter horse track early days. Lukas would listen to his assistants, but he always made the final decisions, while talking on a huge Motorola cell phone with extended antennae attached to his ear, allowing him to coordinate the training plans of over 350 horses at different barns across the country.

The 2-year-old and 3-year-old horses from the Lukas stable were dominating stakes races from coast to coast. Racing young 2-year-old horses remained controversial, and many industry officials didn't believe that 2-year-old thoroughbreds should be raced at all because their bones are not fully developed. But there was big money offered in these races for young stars and Lukas was always to be found where the money showed up. The winning horse owners typically earn 60 percent of the race's purse money, 20 percent for second place, 10 percent for third, five percent for fourth, and three percent for fifth place. Trainers and jockeys usually earn 10 percent each of the winning purse money, and with top races offering a young horse $500,000 or more for under two minutes of racing, the incentives were powerful to get them training and running as early as possible.

Lukas was not in the training game to just win any races. He wanted the big stakes races, the big money offered, and the championship trophies. He was changing the game by flying his horses into any track in the country to take the money and run. A frequent joke on the backstretch was that Lukas horses earned frequent flyer miles. He shipped and won so many stakes races, the gamblers developed a saying: "Bet D. Wayne…off the plane."

Every Lukas barn in every city was laid out in identical ways, allowing horses to be comfortable no matter what track they were flown into; no matter where they bedded down. The barns all featured the same deep hay, same brand of oats, and the hayrack and water buckets were always in the exact same place, allowing a traveling horse to feel at home. Lukas, a former basketball coach, ran his operation like a military unit, with nothing left to chance. Lukas was the first trainer to run his barn like a CEO runs a corporation.

The Lukas barn method dominated the sport, but Lukas was earning a reputation of being out of control with the demands he made of his staff. He insisted on perfection in every detail, including penmanship. He required assistant trainers to improve their handwriting, as reading their notes was a problem for him. He demanded 18-hour workdays of assistant trainers and had them call him at four a.m. and one p.m. daily with updates. There were 87 employees in his employ, and he wanted them to call him immediately, even at midnight, if a horse had an injury or illness.

He said, "I think that the discipline you develop outside the barn and the discipline you develop in your life will carry over into the discipline I need from you in handling the horses and in the stalls. We keep our barns spotless, not because a horse will run any faster if the barn is absolutely spotless, but because that discipline will carry over to what does make a difference. The only thing I really cannot tolerate is a lack of effort. And I don't tolerate that very well with a horse, either. When it gets to that point, I have to say, 'Look, this horse is wasting my time. Let's run him for a claiming tag.'"

Today, Lukas's Winning Colors was going to not waste his time.

Thirty minutes passed quickly, and the horses were being readied for the race. Only five fillies entered the gate for the Grade 1 Las Virgenes Stakes at one-mile, with Winning Colors drawing the number four post position. The entry of the two most respected fillies in America had scared most of the competition away, resulting in a small but talented field.

Klein, his wife Joyce, and guests, were seated at their usual prime turf club table overlooking the finish line. Miami, Dino, and Ava were seated rows above them at their own higher, less well-located table. The attendees at both tables had been down to the paddock to view the fillies as they were being saddled. They'd seen Lukas wearing an elegant blue pinstripe suit and polka dot blue and white silk tie. He had reassembled Winning Colors' white halter before turning her over to Luis. Luis then paraded her in front of the admiring fans, as she bounced with energy while flipping her long mane side to side. The fillies paraded in front of the stands for several minutes before warming up on the backstretch.

Gary Stevens took his perch atop the tall filly and led her to the track to warm up. As she pranced in the warm up, she bit the filly in front of her before Stevens could snatch her head back. Stevens took this as a good sign.

The trumpet player in his bright red formal coat and black top hat played the familiar tune, "Call to the Post."

Dino was very confident of Winning Colors and awaited the moment she'd show the world the future champion he believed she was destined to be. He and Miami had bet $3,000 on her at the windows and were excited and confident of her superiority against the current Eastern champion, Goodbye Halo.

Stevens was concerned about Winning Colors as he led her to the gate. She was clearly unhappy as she threw her head up and to the right. She shied away from the gate the first time he led her to enter. She was agitated—starting and stopping her steps. The jockey spoke to her softly, working to ease her spirits. He noticed that her eyes were darting from the gate to the other fillies as he calmed her. She finally entered the gate quietly.

The crowd was loud as the gates opened. Winning Colors broke forward and seized the lead, but drawn to the inside of her position was the speedy filly Bolchina at 23-1. Winning Colors was fanned, three wide, losing ground into the quick left turn. Bolchina dived inside and challenged the lead with Winning Colors, who, for the first time in her races, was on even terms with another horse in a race. Winning Colors' competitive instinct kicked in and she responded to the challenge as she exploded with speed past Bolchina, sprinting to reestablish herself in front. She'd used considerable energy so early in the race. The two leaders, Winning Colors and Bolchina, were flying on the lead now!

Goodbye Halo was under top national jockey, Jorge Velasquez. He was racing at a relaxed five lengths back from the two leaders, not being asked for more run by Velasquez. The two leading fillies continued dueling on the front end, both wanting the lead.

Bolchina tried but could not get back on even terms with Winning Colors. Stevens suddenly found himself two-and-a-half lengths in front of Bolchina while blasting down the backstretch. Goodbye Halo was relaxed and content several paths outside the rail to let the two other fillies battle for supremacy for the lead down the long Santa Anita backstretch, and then into the start of the stretch turn.

As Winning Colors dove into the start of the far turn, Velasquez asked his mount for run and she willingly accelerated and boldly charged up to within a length behind Winning Colors. For a moment it looked as if Goodbye Halo would rocket past her, but Winning Colors felt Goodbye Halo's presence on her flank, and again with her long strides accelerated to re-open her lead back to a large two-and-a-half length advantage. Winning Colors and Goodbye Halo stormed down the start of the long stretch together. Winning Colors had been asked twice already in the race to stay in front of two challenging, stakes class fillies.

Up in the turf club, Miami and Dino smiled at each other after seeing their gray filly take control over the field. Ava looked like a princess.

The roar of the crowd was so loud, the fillies and jockeys could hear it even over the pounding of the horses' feet into the hard and fast dirt of the track. The expected match race between the two best fillies in the country was on!

The fans encouraged their favorites while those at the Kleins's table shouted, "Keep going!" to Winning Colors.

Dino, normally quiet when watching races, was yelling in a deeper voice than Miami had ever heard in their 15 years of race watching together. "Go baby, go! Go girl…go girl…go girl!"

Goodbye Halo put her head down and dug in, gaining desperate bits of ground with each stride on Winning Colors as they charged together into the stretch run, while distancing the rest of the field. The two champion fillies pulled away from the rest of the field by three, then five, and now eight lengths, up to 30 lengths ahead of the remaining horses.

The race was just between the two star fillies.

Hall of Fame jockey Angel Cordero was watching the battle from the sidelines and later said the race reminded him of the "Ali verses Frazier" boxing ring match.

The two young horses were running full out for their lives as they charged for home, and both dug in; neither would yield to the other. Stevens tried to steer Winning Colors out to the right, trying to race ride her and let her ever so slightly cause Goodbye Halo to not run a straight line. Winning Colors would have no part of it. She darted to the inside, running tucked against and nearly touching the rail, absolutely refusing to quit. Her ears were pinned back while opening again to a length and a half advantage on her foe. Stevens could feel she was tiring and tried to steer her off the rail yet again.

Stevens was thinking about what he'd learned from Winning Colors' two exercise riders that she hated the whip. They'd told him, "Don't whip her. You don't have to…she will give you everything she has. Don't use the whip on her unless you absolutely have to…if you do, she may do something crazy. Gary, really be careful."

Goodbye Halo was not done. She surged back to Winning Colors' side, pinning her against the rail. Stevens reached down and cocked his whip, reached forward and showed it to her, then he reached back, and with some restraint, he used the whip on her for the first time in a race. The sting of Steven's whip continued on his filly as Goodbye Halo was pulling herself forward, in a full-on gallop while inching closer, and closer, racing as a team in unison, side by side, just noses apart.

The wire was close.

Finally, the early demands of sprinting against the speedster Bolchina and fighting off the repeated challenges of Goodbye Halo took its toll on Winning Colors. She was pinned down against the inner rail as Goodbye Halo pulled even and then surged away to a tough, desperate, hard fought, half-length victory at the wire.

The fans were standing and cheering the two gutsy fillies like it was Derby day itself. But the big, gray, Amazon filly was no longer undefeated or invincible.

Miami looked at Dino. He was slumped down in his chair, speechless. His eyes were pointed down at his shoes. He believed in Winning Colors as a world champion and she had not lived up to his dream. He leaned forward to speak, but no words came out.

When Miami turned to look at Ava, he saw that under the brim of her hat, tears were streaming down her face.

CHAPTER 5

The Hotel Impala

Pari-mutuel tickets with zero value were scattered around the table. Dino raised his head, looked at Miami and Ava, and said, "Miami, you know we are the opposite of counterfeiters."

"What the hell are you talking about?"

"Think about it. What do counterfeiters do? They turn worthless paper into money," said Dino as he picked up a stack of losing Winning Colors tickets and threw the stack high into the air like confetti. "What we do is take money and turn it into worthless paper."

"You're not helping," Miami replied. He motioned to the waiter then ordered two Bacardi and Cokes for them and a glass of chardonnay for Ava. They were now officially on a major losing streak, and not just because of Winning Colors. The day before, they'd lost three consecutive race photo finishes. That same week, they'd accumulated over a dozen other losing race bets. They were down much more than the $5,000 bet they'd placed in Tijuana.

The question of whether Winning Colors would even be entered in the Derby came up in conversation. "Why would Lukas and Klein enter her against the boys if she can't even beat the best of the girls?" Miami asked then added, "But the Derby's not for another two months, so she still has time to regroup. Let's hope she'll rebound. Dino we need to rebound, too. We're getting killed at the windows."

Ava asked, "If she doesn't run in the Derby, what happens to the money you bet on her?"

"They keep it, and we get second jobs at McDonalds," said Dino.

The next morning, Miami called Dino early to say, "I'm thinking it's time for a change of scenery, buddy. I hear the desert is nice this time of year. Where could we go to in the desert?"

"You thinking like the Hoover Dam? Or some museums? If we go, we need to make reservations."

"Viva Las Vegas, baby! You worry too much, buddy. Vegas is just one giant hotel room. No problem ever getting a room. They have more rooms there than people to fill them, but I'll take care of it. Don't worry about a thing except your liver."

"OK. I can call in sick."

"Yeah baby! Vegas. Ava's traveling on business anyway. I've traded Ava for you… it's not the best trade…but let's do this!"

Later that afternoon, Dino picked up Miami in the Impala. Miami had the much nicer car, but it was not the best vehicle for the five-hour drive to Las Vegas from Los Angeles. The boys were far bigger bettors on horses than on the Las Vegas gaming tables, but still liked to take a flyer at the craps table with all the yelling and screaming of the hopeful bettors. Miami was doing the driving and had hit 96 mph though the desert, anxious to get a first cocktail under his belt.

Dino looked scared and his eyes looked like they were bulging because of the lenses of his wide glasses. "I don't mind gambling, but is an older Chevy Impala supposed to go 100 miles an hour?"

"There's nothing to worry about, as long as I keep my hands firmly on the wheel at all times." Miami hit the gas harder, took his hands off the wheel…and showed them both to Dino.

Dino couldn't see that Miami was steering with his knees on the wheel. He screamed, "You're going to get us killed! Stop it. Goddamn it!"

Miami backed the speed back down to 90 mph, mostly because he was laughing too hard to drive properly. They got to the Strip in four hours and 30 minutes.

They arrived in Las Vegas, parked the car, and walked into The Mandalay Bay Hotel to go straight to the Sports and Race Book to see the odds offered on Winning Colors to win the Derby. They were surprised to see only 12-1 offered, after her loss the day before, but they also knew that futures book odds tend to only go down after good races and not up much in odds after poor prep races.

Next, they visited the craps tables. Miami bet far more than Dino, which was the opposite of their norm at the track where Dino would often bet three or four times more than him. Miami liked to bet and party, but Dino liked to bet to win money, and a random bet at a craps table offered him no insider's edge that he believed he had at the racetrack when he was betting against the other horse players, and not betting against the house like at the casino.

After they lost a few hundred dollars at the craps table, they headed over to the lobby to get a room.

"Sorry sir, we're all sold out for the convention," said the desk clerk.

Dino said, "Miami, you said you would take care of a reservation. Please…tell me you made a backup reservation at Caesars Palace. They always take care of me."

"No worries mate, we'll get a great room. They love you at Caesars Palace. We've seen it every time."

The two men left the Mandalay and went to the place they felt represented everything that was great—and also wrong—about Las Vegas. This hotel has towering Roman statues and gaudy columns that allow it to morph from garish to classy. The fountains in the front of Caesars Palace set the heart of every gambler fluttering the moment they head down the long entrance driveway. For two Los Angelinos used to seeing Rodeo Drive, this place made Beverly Hills look like Topeka, Kansas.

Dino noticed the décor and asked, "Miami, what the fuck do white statues of prancing horses and angels blowing trumpets have to do with gambling?"

"I think those are all gambling images going back to the Bible or something. Those early Bible people really liked to gamble. That's why they invented chariots. Chariot gambling was big back then."

"Yeah…I would have probably been a professional chariot racing gambler back then."

Unfortunately, despite Dino being on their comped players list, there were no rooms at this inn, either. People in for a food convention had taken over the town. The concierge was sympathetic, but said, "Mr. D, if you had called ahead I'm sure we could have arranged something nice for you."

Miami and Dino hit the craps table to regroup. There they ran into one of Dino's appraisal clients. Working all day then flying to Vegas for the night was common for this guy. Dino placed small bets on the table next to the client and the dice began to get hot for them. The client asked Dino, "Where are you staying in Vegas?"

"You wouldn't know it. It's smaller hotel just outside of town."

"I know this town really well. What's it called?"

"The Hotel Impala. Small place…yellow…very intimate…off the main drag."

"Yeah…we have two separate suites," added Miami.

The boys played a few hours longer, lost about $250 each, and were zombie-level tired. Miami could no longer keep his eyes open and told Dino he needed to sleep. It was now after two a.m., and after driving and casino hopping for 12 hours both men were inebriated, exhausted… and had neither room nor bed.

Miami went to the pay phone and called every hotel outside of the Strip. When he gave it up, he said, "Dino, let's just sleep a couple of hours in your car until the morning and then I'm sure we'll find a ton of rooms when some people check out."

It became their plan. They found a well-lit parking space behind a cheap casino and tried to sleep, but with no blankets or pillows, they were cold and uncomfortable. It was 36 degrees Fahrenheit outside the car…a cold, windy, winter Las Vegas night.

Miami had an idea. "Let's turn on the car heater for 15 minutes. I'll stay up until it warms up and then turn it off."

Dino was not having it. "No friggin' way! I know we'll fall asleep and die of carbon monoxide poisoning. It'll be the perfect ending to a perfect weekend."

"Don't worry, man, I'll stay up. Remember I used to be a long-distance sailor and can sit a damn watch for 15 damn minutes. I'm trained for this. Buddy…look it's four a.m. now, at 4:20 I'll turn off the car and sleep. You take the back suite…seat."

Dino gave in, nodded off, and was soon snoring.

At 6:00 a.m. Miami was smacked in the face with a folded racing program. "What the hell! You said you would stay up and turn off the car. We could have died in this cheap, dumpy casino's parking lot."

"Sorry. Sorry, man. I guess I dozed off, too. But hey, we are OK! We're alive! We broke our losing streak! Come on, breakfast is on me."

"The rest of my life is on you."

They had breakfast at the same Denny's Luis and his buddies dined at two months earlier and then cruised to Caesars Palace to plead for a room. They got one but were told they could not check in until after two p.m. Relieved, they pulled from their small suitcases toothbrushes, toothpaste, deodorant, one hairbrush, and some hair spray. In the marble ambiance of the men's room, Miami and Dino spent a good 20 minutes manscaping.

"You don't look much like Don Johnson now," said Dino talking to the mirror image of his friend. "That cotton teal sports coat looks more like a wrinkled dinner napkin than a 'Miami Vice' jacket."

Dino's hair was sticking straight up, but only in parts. "Yeah," said Miami, "and you look like those guys that play in the band Devo."

Two other men were brushing their teeth. "See…this is no big deal," Miami said in a whisper.

Dino threw the can of hair spray at him. It missed Miami's head and tumbled, clanging, across the floor. "Stop speaking to me. Ever."

They left the restroom and headed to place bets at the race book on East Coast horse races. Dino did well and won a photo finish on an 8-1 shot at Gulfstream Park racetrack in Hallandale Beach, Florida. That win got them both nearly back in the black.

At 1:00 p.m., they checked with the desk and learned a room was ready. They were escorted to a nice suite, not a full high roller penthouse, but an upgraded view room on an upper level floor, stocked with champagne and liquor. Dino tipped the bellman two bucks. Miami noticed the pissed look on his face and handed him $10 more when Dino wasn't paying attention.

"Now we're talking, Dino. I told you we'd get rooms!"

"We? We, kimosabe? We didn't get us a room. I got us a damn room."

"No…you got us a roof view suite, baby!"

Miami popped open a chilled bottle of French champagne and poured two glasses. "Why is it that free liquor always tastes better?"

They made reservations for dinner at nine p.m. at the Bacchanal gourmet restaurant, and then took naps.

Upon waking, Miami hit the electric shades on the living room window and the bright Las Vegas Strip lights came into full view. The iconic round towers of the Sands Hotel were dwarfed by the huge Bally's sign touting Dean Martin as headliner, with Sammy Davis Jr. noted as coming soon. The Frontier featured Siegfried and Roy, and the Desert Inn highlighted Crystal Gayle. Miami loved the Desert Inn, as he had hung out with Howard Cosell at the bar one night there, and it had a smaller, classy feel to it.

"What do you think...should we bring Ava and Amalia here?" asked Miami.

"We have never even thought about bringing girlfriends to Vegas."

"I don't know...I think Ava would love the lights of the Strip."

The conversation ended without any resolution as they dressed for dinner.

Dino and Miami were escorted to a VIP table and opened huge menus the size of small desks. They ordered another bottle of French champagne, appetizers, and then a 1975 George Latour, B.V. Estate, Cabernet Sauvignon, along with bone-in, prime aged steaks, mushrooms, and Florentine stuffed potatoes.

"Just like the Hotel Impala...huh, buddy?" Miami said, between bites.

"Not quite...I miss the carbon monoxide and you snoring. Man, this is what it was probably like to be Frank Sinatra every night of his life."

Seeing an opening for more serious conversation, Miami told Dino that things were getting serious with he and Ava.

"I'm glad for you, but does this mean you won't be going to the track much? Name one guy we know that goes to the track three times per week who is married or has a steady girlfriend."

"Nothing will change, my brother. Maybe I won't go on her birthday and stuff."

Despite the great meal, and being with his best friend, Miami felt lonely. He wanted to share the meal with Ava and take her to a show. Or, maybe just sit in the lounge with her and listen to the singers. Then again, why mess it up by getting married? I love my life, he thought. Still, a couple of my own baby fillies and colts could be cool too...one day.

When the check came, all that was required was for Dino to sign the comp slip, and Miami put down a $100 bill as a tip. They went to the tables looking for a hot craps pit. Craps was their game; it had the best odds for the players, and they always played the same way. They limited losses to $100 each at each table and played aggressively. If they won, they increased their bets, and kept pressing if they were hitting some numbers. Their number one rule was to never chase. If either lost $100, they'd move on to another table. Playing by this method, they knew being "hot" could mean a lot of cash; going "cold" wouldn't hurt much.

After several hours of rolling dice, drinking free cocktails, and losing about $500 each, Miami and Dino went over to the vast, now empty Sports Book about two a.m. They sat down under the giant odds boards in comfortable, oversized, light brown leather chairs. The Caesars Palace Sports Book was nirvana to them, and they smiled at each other, now at total peace with their world. This location was the center of each man's personal universe.

Miami thought it was like the way Ansel Adams felt when hiking in the wilderness, or how Mark Spitz felt about swimming. "You know Dino, most people are unhappy because they never find out what they really like. They are always searching and traveling to find out what will make them happy. You and I knew the first time we set foot into a racetrack. Me, it was Hollywood Park at age 14."

"For me, it was Santa Anita at age four."

"We are lucky men."

"Damn right we are," said Miami as they sat staring at the odds for the Super Bowl, the coming NBA summer playoffs, and tomorrow's odds for the horse races from California to Florida.

"Can we live here?" Dino asked.

After two nights in Vegas, Dino had to be back in Los Angeles by Tuesday evening. Miami as usual woke up early, despite going to bed after three a.m. He missed Ava and hoped to see her that night when he got home. He knew she was at a trade show in San Francisco, knew the hotel where she was staying, and knew she planned to take the one-hour flight home that same afternoon. He called the hotel and asked for Ms. Bouchon's room. It was eight a.m. The phone rang eight times, and he hung up.

After three minutes, he called again. After the fourth ring, he heard noises...it sounded like the phone had been dropped. Then more noises. A man's sleepy, gravelly voice mumbled, "Yeah...what?"

He heard Ava say, "Who is it?"

Miami was uncertain what to do...or say. He felt like an idiot for missing her...while being in Vegas, for Christ's sake. "Tell her it's Mark."

He hung up.

Dino and Miami grabbed two large coffees at the breakfast bar, fortified with three Tylenols each, headed straight to the Impala, and hit the long open road back to Los Angeles.

The first three hours of driving were quiet. Miami knew Dino wasn't used to being hung over. He didn't feel like talking anyway. He thought of telling Dino about Ava but didn't feel up to sharing it, and Dino was still pissed off at him because of the hassle with travel arrangements.

Dino started laughing. He said that he'd totaled the combined hours of sleep they had accomplished in the past 48 hours. The number was less than seven! "And we look like roadkill."

About 90 miles southwest of Vegas, they stopped at the run-down Bun Boy coffee shop in Baker, California. Miami told Dino, "Baker is not the end of the world, but you can see it from here. Look at that sign. We are only two miles from The World's Largest Thermometer, which is Baker's only apparent claim to fame, other than us dining here at the world-famous Bun Boy. The end to a perfect fucking day."

Dino pulled his head up and squinted at Miami. He waited a bit then asked him, "What's wrong, man?"

"Nothing. I'm just tired. We can talk about it later."

"OK. Well, what about going to Santa Anita next week?"

"I'll skip it," said Miami. He didn't really want to rule it out, but he also didn't want to commit to going with Dino after the time they'd just spent in Vegas.

"Me too," Dino concurred.

Three hours later, Dino dropped Miami off at his condominium, and then arrived a bit later at his apartment in Santa Monica.

CHAPTER 6

Girls Don't Belong

Three days after Winning Colors' first career loss to Goodbye Halo, the whooping sound of helicopter blades startled the horses. It was in the early morning and Lukas had just flown in on the new private Sikorsky helicopter acquired in partnership with Klein. Lukas and Klein were meeting at Lukas's office in Rancho Santa Fe to discuss plans for her next start.

Klein did not look well. He seemed to have aged rapidly since their last meeting, and his hair had turned completely white. Something was wrong. Lukas realized Klein was no longer flying in to watch his horses run in the big East Coast stakes races. Instead, Klein had been flying to Las Vegas to watch in an air-conditioned casino on wide screen TV. Lukas was worried for his friend's health and was aware that he might lose his best client.

Lukas asked Luis to come into his track office to give a report to Klein. Luis told them both that Winning Colors was in good shape. Sometimes, after a hard-fought loss, a horse will go off their feed and become listless, but Winning Colors apparently had no memory of her loss. She bounced back as feisty as ever. That morning, when Luis called to her, Winning Colors went for his shirt pockets with her muzzle and bit through his clothing, as if insisting he must have some treats for her hidden somewhere. When she couldn't find a treat, she lowered her head and threw it up at him, tossing him backwards like a rag doll. He found two sugar cubes in his jean pockets and held them under her nose. She chomped them down and proceeded to bite through his shirt pocket looking for more.

Klein shook Luis' hand, and while thanking him for the great job he'd been doing with her, handed him three $100 bills.

Luis tried to give him back the money and said, "Señor, no es necesario," but the owner insisted, and Luis smiled as he tucked the bills in the torn pocket of his work shirt. The bonus was nearly one week's pay to Luis, and he knew they appreciated what he was doing for her.

After Luis left the meeting, Lukas told Klein, "Let's just bring her right back at Halo in the Santa Anita Oaks."

"Do whatever you want, buy what you want, run 'em where you want," Klein responded, "but if you start losing my money, I'll jerk the rug out from you."

The Oaks was the biggest race for 3-year-old fillies of the meet, now just two weeks away. Lukas was famous for working and running his horses hard. The legendary trainer Charles Whittingham had told Lukas, "Racehorses are like bananas. They spoil quickly," so Lukas believed in running them when they were healthy. Despite being the most successful trainer in the world, Lukas felt he hadn't received the credit he deserved. At every venue he had ever trained, from the cheap, quarter horse tracks in Oklahoma, Kansas, or New Mexico, or the big sprint tracks like Los Alamitos, he had been hugely successful. In 10 years, he had made the transition from quarter horse trainer to be the winningest thoroughbred trainer in America.

Klein asked, "Wayne, can she still beat the boys?"

"Damn straight she can," Lukas replied. "I checked the times of her races and she is running faster than the colts. Goodbye Halo ran her eyeballs out to beat your girl, but remember, Halo had much more experience and seasoning. Your filly will know what to expect next time and will rip Halo's heart out."

Lukas never lacked for enthusiasm. The top quarter horse jockey, Bobby Adair, said of Lukas, "I want to die the same day as Lukas. Because no matter how I screw up before I die, if I arrive at the Pearly Gates with Lukas, I know for sure he can talk the both of us in."

What Lukas didn't know was that Luis was a bit worried that Lukas was training her too hard. Fillies are usually not able to handle the training workload of a mature male thoroughbred, and she was just a 3-year-old, early in her career, with only four starts. Winning Colors became agitated if she wasn't galloped hard every day by Dallas Stewart, her exercise rider.

Dallas met with Luis in the late afternoon. "Luis…do you understand? She is getting too high strung for me to handle her in the mornings. I need to be the first rider out with her the moment the track opens for training at 5:00 a.m., when there's less horse traffic, less noise, and fewer horses for her to attack. She seems to especially be going after the older mares if they get in her way on the way to the track."

Luis replied, "They need to stay out of her way, but I will have her ready every morning."

Winning Colors was thriving and getting taller and more muscular each month. The other grooms and trainers would come to see her and always left shaking their heads, amazed how big and tall she was. Around the backstretch, she was known as the Amazon.

From 5:00 a.m. each day, Santa Anita was alive and active as the sun rose over the backstretch, silhouetting the mountains. As the exercise riders took out their charges for jogs or serious workouts, the horses' warm, moist breaths could be seen exploding into the cold winter air. Continuing to teach Winning Colors how to reserve and rate her energy remained Jeff Lukas's primary training focus with her each morning. Dallas would position her to run slightly behind another horse and remain there for a half-mile, coaching her to relax before running at her full-speed gallop. Then, in the stretch, he would allow her to accelerate and exert her superiority over her workmate.

Occasionally, Gary Stevens showed up to ride her in the early workouts. The two had a bond. After a few weeks of working together, Winning Colors showed excitement when she saw Stevens, knowing she would soon escape her stall and gallop around the huge track. He told Jeff Lukas, "I'm beginning to understand her now. She seems to be going too fast early in her training and in races…but she just has an ability to go faster out of the gate than any other horse I have ever been on. We just need to keep her head on straight. If she gets distracted or angry she goes out of whack and then you can't control her. It's only her temperament I worry about…never her ability."

After her daily morning exercise, Luis would take her for a long walk, and then give her a slow, warm bath, combing her out afterwards until she shone like a new metallic gray sports car. Horsemen know they shouldn't get too attached to their horses, but Luis couldn't help himself.

Jeff Lukas aspired to run his own stable someday, and he found a willing business mentor in Eugene Klein. The two often dined together at a famous Santa Anita steak house, founded in 1922, The Derby. The Saturday evening before Winning Colors' next start, Klein took Jeff out for drinks and steaks. Jeff had learned that after a few cocktails, Klein would tell colorful stories of his rise to wealth.

Early in his career, Klein had been known as Cowboy Gene, but he wasn't really a cowboy. At a towering six-feet-five-inches, he was a gangly kid from the Bronx born to Russian immigrants, who sold encyclopedias door to door as a kid. He was a cocky, brash, and gutsy salesman who parlayed a used car lot with three cheap cars into a Volvo automobile dealership, created a national movie chain with 250 theaters, built an NBA franchise, owned an insurance and banking company, and then leveraged himself into his long-held dream of owning a professional football team. Klein began his career in sales by running Sunday used car commercials on TV while donning a huge cowboy hat and cowboy boots. The persona of Cowboy Gene was a hit, and he never stopped making money from there.

"I may have been the first Jewish cowboy," he used to say.

"What was it like owning your own NFL team?"

"Initially, I loved it. It had been my dream, even when I owned the Seattle SuperSonics, but I really wanted a football team. But it wasn't what I expected. For instance...they couldn't seem to grow grass in our San Diego stadium. How can they not grow decent grass in Southern California, but they can do it in friggin' Green Bay? Then things went downhill fast for me...." He stopped telling his story to order another Macallan 21, then continued. "The players caused problems."

"Off the field?"

"One day head coach Don Coryell came to me and said, 'Mr. Klein we have a big problem with Jones.'"

Klein took a sip and went on, "I tell him, 'We always have a problem with Jones. What the hell is it now?' Coryell tells me Jones won't play unless I give him a Cadillac. Says he is as important to the team as the owner and the owner drives a Cadillac and he needs one too. We had been dealing with Jones' erratic behavior for two years, but this was a new twist. The thing is Jones was one of the best running backs in the league and without him, we had no chance to win the game. So I tell him, 'Coach, what do you think we should do? Is he serious about this or just Jones being Jones again?'"

Lukas kept quiet. He knew Klein trusted him with these kinds of stories.

"Coach tells me, 'Boss, I hate to say this, but I really don't think he will play if he doesn't get that car. And I know you don't want to hear this again, but he really is underpaid.'"

Klein shifted in his seat and leaned forward. "Well, I had a well-earned reputation of never re-negotiating a contract. But, after years of failure on the field, I needed that weekend's win. I was really getting pissed. I said, 'Coach, I'm friggin' paying him what he friggin' signed up to play for…for God's sakes. I have run businesses from car dealerships to theater chains. Never once did one of my goddamn employees come to me and demand to have a new expensive car delivered to him immediately or he wouldn't come to work the next day! God damn him!'"

"So what happened?"

"I gave in…bought him a new baby blue, Landau top Cadillac, with silver chrome wheels. Jones ran for 110 yards that weekend, but we lost the damn game anyway."

Klein finished his drink and ordered another.

"What made you finally sell the team?"

"So many damn things. The press was always against us. The agents knew how to spin it and make me look bad. They'd heard Dan Fouts wanted to stay in San Diego, but I wouldn't pay him. And I was paying him…exactly what his contract said he should be paid! The absolute worst agent was Howard Slusher. We called him Agent Orange because of his hair and his personality. It started bad for him! Slusher tried re-negotiating the contract for the league's leading receiver, John Jefferson. The contract was $100,000 per year, plus friggin' incentives that had paid him an additional $85,000 in the same year. I got pissed and told our general manger to trade him the next day to Green Bay! I was just sending a message to all the other players. If you want to play in sunny San Diego for the Chargers, honor your damn contract!"

"What would you tell the agents when they tried to re-negotiate their existing contacts?"

"That was the fun part! I would just tell 'em, 'If he doesn't want to play, I wish him a great deal of luck in his new career, whatever it might be!'"

After their meal of thick steaks, Klein paid the check and looked at Jeff. He said, "Probably it was the NFL owners that finally made me just want to sell. Some of these damn owners never did anything right in their lives except inherit their parents' money. They didn't think like businessmen, they didn't act like businessmen, and they didn't care if they made money! Al Davis is a total jerk."

"Racing's gain, Mr. Klein."

"Really Jeff, it was Joyce who got me to sell the team and introduced me to your dad. He and I are really quite alike, Jeff...afraid of nothing!"

March 13, 1988, Santa Anita Racetrack, California

Even though the sky was overcast on the day of the Santa Anita Oaks race, the fans came pouring into the track early to get prime viewing spots for what was being called a match race. There were only four horses running. Most fans now believed that Goodbye Halo was a superhorse and she was being selected to win by most of the newspaper handicappers. Dino and Miami had gone to their good friend, racing author, and professional handicapper, Jay Quest, for his race insights. Quest had written several of the most respected handicapping books in the industry, and they valued his opinions.

When asked about Goodbye Halo versus Winning Colors, Quest told them, "I have often seen top fast fillies; when they are first challenged in a race by another top-class filly, they may fail quite badly in that race. But I usually have seen them bounce back from the experience and run the best races of their young lives next time. I think Winning Colors just has too much talent as evidenced by her blazing early speed. Boys, stay with Colors, and good luck with your Mexico bet."

"I hope we're not going to be rich dead men from the cartel guys," Miami told Quest.

Racetrack bettors are almost always thought of as colorful characters with nicknames like, well, Miami. Many teachers, professors, and individuals interested in mathematics are drawn to horseracing. Studying a *Daily Racing Form's* past performance newspaper, and then projecting out a race's winner, was an academic challenge for many extremely educated and bright people like Quest.

Miami and Dino's handicapping hero was a former college professor, Tim Raymond. Tim taught them how to use numbers to estimate how fast horses would likely race, while going different distances they had not previously run. He had helped both Dino and Miami have many of their biggest winning days. When Miami asked Tim what he thought of Winning Colors' race day chances, Tim replied, "Colors is better than Halo. Keep the faith."

The fans came to bet Goodbye Halo back off her win, and she was bet down to solid favoritism, well below even money. That day's Stakes was run at one-and-one-sixteenth miles, a sixteenth of a mile farther than their previous race together. This made fans and gamblers believe that more distance could only help Goodbye Halo's late charge. Meanwhile, Winning Colors was being relatively ignored in the betting in the four-horse race; she was offered at over 2-1 odds in the short field.

Other top fillies were reluctant to race against the big two horses for fear of being embarrassed. Dino and Miami were now very respectful of Goodbye Halo's winning chances in the championship filly race, but at the current odds, they believed Winning Colors was a steal.

"I feel like we already have $5,000 to win on her because of our Mexico bet, and today is do-or-die for the Derby. Still, at 2-1, we have to bet more on her," Dino said as they went to the large transaction windows, betting $2,000 to win on today's race.

Luis was smiling as he led Winning Colors into the saddling paddock. His filly was dramatically taller and bigger, by nearly 200 pounds, than the other young fillies. She walked around the saddling enclosure in front of the fans, now five persons deep, trying to get a look at the two-star fillies.

Goodbye Halo was trained by a man nicknamed "The Bald Eagle" Charles Whittingham, a Hall of Fame trainer, and ridden again by Pat Day, a star veteran jockey with more experience than Gary Stevens, who once again was piloting Klein's gray filly. When Winning Colors saw Goodbye Halo, she became agitated and snorted. She whirled repeatedly on her hindquarters, trying to break away from Luis' firm hand on her lead. He had not seen her like this before a race and was worried she would break free or use up her energy before the race had begun. The fans tried to be quiet to not startle the horses, but they were still loud as they strained to see their favorites.

The steward announced, "Riders up," a signal to the trainers to give a leg up to the jockeys on the four fillies. The fans roared when the horses entered to parade in front of the grandstand and began their warm ups. The gray lady settled down for Stevens as soon as he gave her the freedom to canter down the backstretch in her pre-race warm up routine.

Dino and Miami knew that Winning Colors had to win this race, or she would not make the Kentucky Derby, period. She was still not the fan's betting favorite. More than three times as much was bet on Goodbye Halo than Winning Colors.

The four fillies entered the starting gate. At the bell, both star fillies broke like bullets out of a gun, with Winning Colors being sent to the lead by Stevens as they ripped into the left-hand first turn. Stevens didn't have to ask her to run as Winning Colors was cruising at a high rate of speed on her own courage. She opened up down the backstretch by three lengths while running next to the rail, as Goodbye Halo was pushed by Pat Day to not let her get away.

Both Goodbye Halo and the filly Jeanne Jones took up the chase and got nearly on even terms with Winning Colors. Goodbye Halo was squeezed for a moment and bobbled slightly, between Jeanne Jones and Winning Colors. It looked for a moment like Goodbye Halo would be forced to take up, but she was spirited and gunned forward through the smallest of openings by Day until the two-star fillies now were head to head. Their jockeys pushed their charges forward harder. They quickly put away Jeanne Jones, who fell back as the two favorites engaged much earlier than in the previous race when Goodbye Halo waited to charge late in the stretch to her victory. Goodbye Halo was trying to beat Winning Colors at her own game, with blazing early speed!

Gary Stevens looked a full head higher than Pat Day and the other jockeys as he thrust his hands aggressively forward into her gray mane. The beautiful animal responded by lengthening all of her long, full body into the first turn. The interior quarter- and half-mile fractions set were wickedly fast, much faster than they had set in their last match when Winning Colors tired and faded to second.

Miami saw the quarter-mile and half-mile fractions blink on the tote board, 22-and-two-fifths and 44-and-four-fifths seconds and shouted to Dino over the crowd noise, "They are going way too damn fast for the distance! Those are sprinters' fractions. Can they go that fast and survive? They could both get beat by the closers."

Winning Colors edged away just slightly. Goodbye Halo was pushed by her jockey, now urging his filly with his arms. He was asking her to pick up the pace and not let the gray filly steal away from her. Goodbye Halo dug back in and lowered her head in determination, trying valiantly to stay with the gray filly, but Day could tell she could not match strides with Winning Colors. The early fractions had cooked Goodbye Halo from the inside, as she could not sustain such a fast pace. As she tired, Stevens sensed now was the time to take command of the race. He was hand riding Winning Colors, urging her on, chirping to her, "Go girl… go girl." He never touched his whip. Winning Colors pulled away from Goodbye Halo by four, then five, then seven, then eight dominating lengths as she annihilated the field strung out behind her. Goodbye Halo was now exhausted from trying to keep pace with the huge gray filly; she was caught for second, beaten by an astounding 10 lengths to the wire by Winning Colors.

Stevens raised his whip triumphantly at the wire!

Luis was beaming as he grabbed her halter minutes later and led her panting and glistening with sweat, for her winner's photo with the jubilant party of Klein, Joyce, and friends. A thoroughbred racehorse after a race has capillaries fully engaged with blood, and with her veins standing out on her long, tall, silver-gray shining body, Winning Colors was a beautiful and intimidating 1,200-pound glorious, but sweaty animal.

Lukas was ecstatic as he held the heavy silver Santa Anita Oaks trophy over his head with two hands. Now he was sure there was truly a superhorse in his barn.

Miami and Dino were jubilant as they watched the owners celebrate in the winner's circle and accept the Santa Anita Oaks 1988 trophy.

Dino said, "One more California victory against the colts next month and she'll qualify for the Kentucky Derby! The Santa Anita Derby is next. Look at Mr. Klein. If he is ever going to win the Derby, he has to do it soon."

"Super Dino, you are right," Miami said. "I think the only trainer in all of California that would run her against the best males in the country is Lukas. He is not afraid to beat the boys with girls, and Winning Colors is just faster than them. I really believe that now, too. Dino you were right, baby! Please Mr. Lukas, tell us soon she will go against the boys in the Santa Anita Derby and then on to the Kentucky Derby!"

They found out two days later that Klein and Lukas had entered Winning Colors in both the Kentucky Oaks and the Kentucky Derby. The owner and trainer were keeping their options open as to where she should run next.

Dino and Miami still had to sweat out getting their girl into the big dance.

Late the following Wednesday night, Dino got a call from his favorite librarian. What she told him made him sit down and become seriously afraid for their lives. The Tijuana reporter who'd been reporting on Jorge Hank Rhon, El Gato, had been targeted. The windows of his office had been shattered by machine gun fire. Apparently writing articles on Rhon and associated cartel figures was infuriating for those being written about and they sent him a terrifying message with a hail of gunfire. El Gato was not at the office and was unharmed. The journalist was certain that the cartel was sending him a message to stop writing negative articles on Rhon.

Dino called Miami. "I admit it. I'm too damn scared to go back to Agua Caliente. Especially if we are going back there to pick up $250,000 in cash. I'm afraid of the track's owner, and his friends, the guards, everyone. Who can we trust there, man? They are shooting their machine guns out in the open. Maybe they pay us, and then five minutes later have someone rob us in the parking lot, or they kidnap us."

Ever the optimist, Miami said, "I hope we have that problem to face, buddy."

CHAPTER 7

Heaven

All racetracks are unusual places. On any given day, the turf club could be filled with some of the wealthiest people in the country watching their own personal horses compete. At England's top track, Royal Ascot Racecourse, the Queen of England frequently attends to view her own horses run. English gentlemen will be found wearing top hats and tuxedoes, while the ladies sport elegant dresses, custom hats, and fine jewelry.

However, at the same tracks, on the same days, the grandstand is filled with people from all walks of life, some at the lowest economic levels, who survive on welfare and other forms of government assistance. In between the exclusive private spaces and the open-air seating is the clubhouse, filled with middle-class fans. It's a truth that diverse groups love the sport of horse racing.

Miami understood it. He believed that to buy a betting ticket on a horse, for the minutes of that race, the gambler owns that horse's performance as well as a potential to gain the joy of a profit or experience the sting of a loss. "Greatest game in the world!" he always said about it. Someday I'll bring my sons here, he often thought. "Other dads will take their kids to the playground, but I'll bring mine to Hollywood Park, and Santa Anita Park!"

All racetrack venues are not equal. Most tracks today show the evidence that they were built in a bygone era. In the late 1930s, over 40,000 fans would attend Seabiscuit's workouts, and for his great match race against War Admiral, over 40 million people listened on the radio. The great tracks of Saratoga Race Course in New York, and Churchill

Downs in Kentucky, were built in 1863 and 1875. A bit later, Belmont Park in New York was built in 1905, and Santa Anita Park, in Southern California, was constructed in 1934. These places were built in the era before televised Super Bowls, or March Madness college basketball playoffs. They were built when the two most popular US spectator sports were boxing and horseracing. These magnificent tracks were built when land was plentiful, and the track grounds could accommodate over 100,000 fans during the top races. Walking through these old racetracks is like walking through history, and, except for the fashions of the men and women in attendance, the grounds are not much different today than they were 100 years ago.

Miami believed that the track, Las Vegas casinos, and other forms of gambling were not intrinsically evil. Nor was drinking alcohol intrinsically evil...in his view. People go to a two-day Las Vegas getaway, lose their allocated $500 bankroll, and then go back to be a teacher, realtor, or an accountant the next Monday morning. In the same way, most people can drink a couple of beers or glasses of wine at happy hour, and report back to work the next day without any issues. For about five percent of the population, moderation is impossible and they drink or gamble to excess. Yet, there's a perception that if you like to hang out at the track and take chances on a bet or two (or three), you're seen as a social deviant. Some people talk about baseball's Wrigley Field like it was a shrine or a museum, but they think of racetracks as one step above brothels.

For decades, horseracing and movie stars seem to have been attracted to one another on the big weekend stakes days. In contrast, the only celebrities that Miami and Dino saw with some regularity on weekdays at the track were Farah Fawcett, Walter Matthau, Don Adams, and comedian Tim Conway. Matthau basically lived at the track when not filming and often said, "The best thing in the world is winning at the racetrack. The second greatest thing in the world...is losing at the racetrack." Fawcett loved riding horses and was a real race fan. Adams and Conway hung out at the track all the time and to Miami they were a real life "odd couple."

Most horseplayers lose money at the track, but Conway found the humor in it. On one occasion, Miami, Dino, and Conway rode down the turf club elevator that was full of losing horseplayers at the end of the gambling day. Everyone was silent until Conway said, "Anyone want to buy a rental car?"

Once asked how he did at the track that day. Conway quipped, "I had a $300 hot dog."

The Kentucky Derby, referred to as "The Greatest Two Minutes in Sports", a race between 3-year-old horses, is one of the most celebrated sports events of all time. It is always run on the first Saturday in May and has been since 1875. In the 113 Derbies between 1875 and 1987, only two female horses won the race. The odds of a filly winning this race are astronomical. The Kentucky Derby is truly a once-in-a-lifetime shot for any 3-year-old horse with ability.

Now the 3-year-old filly Winning Colors was about to tackle the colts in one of the top qualifying races, the $500,000 purse Santa Anita Derby.

Because the backstretch at the track is a bastion of employment of males (95 percent of all trainers and jockeys are men), Winning Colors was being belittled for being female. The field of sports is a wonderful meritocracy, and gamblers and odds makers are the best evaluators of talent.

The day of the Santa Anita Derby, the track's morning line odds maker had the gray Amazon filly not even listed as the favorite, but rather the second betting choice at 2.5-1. She was in a tough field of nine horses for the prestigious California version of the Kentucky Derby.

Part of this chauvinism was driven by the economics of racing. The winner of a Grade 1 stakes race such as the Santa Anita Derby, and especially the Kentucky Derby, increases the breeding price of the winning stallion by tens of thousands of dollars per mare. With a top stallion able to be bred 200 or more times per year at a fee sometimes exceeding $100,000 per breeding, many trainers and owners felt it was a waste to have a filly win such a race. She could produce only one foal per year verses a male who could produce up to 200 new runners per year.

Eugene Klein opened up to his wife about a specific concern: "Joyce, I never won a Super Bowl. Will I live to win a Derby?"

"Honey, I want you to lose a few pounds, and stop drinking. That would be a start." Joyce Klein was concerned about her husband's poor health and heart condition. She was also worried about who besides Gene could handle the businesses (and especially the costs) of running the large number of horses they now owned together. "I wanted you to sell the football team so you could relax and go to the races with me on the weekends. I never dreamed you would buy hundreds of racehorses… and your own private training facility. Who would buy 250 acres of the most expensive San Diego real estate and then put horses on it? I should have known…you will never slow down."

"I play to win. You know that."

"But what if you can't run this? I don't know how to run a horse farm. How many horses do you have? Tell me the truth, Gene."

Klein paused. He knew that he had perhaps gone off the deep end into the horse business. With the cost of keeping a horse in training at $25,000 per year, he had not expected to get the bills he was now paying. He owned over 150 racehorses. They were not all in full training at the same time, but his training bills were over $300,000 per month, plus the real estate expenses on his Del Rayo Racing Stables farm, near his Rancho Santa Fe estate.

"We have like 100 horses," Eugene said to Joyce. "Did you see the one I just named after the Raiders' owner, Al Davis…Contempt? That's worth the cost! Joyce…you're not so good at saving money either I've noticed. How many people did you invite to the party last year in the back yard?"

"Five hundred."

"Did that include the 16-piece full orchestra? Oh, what the hell… we can afford it!"

Joyce told him, "I think we should sell the ranch, and most of the horses. Gene, think about me, and the kids. What are we going to do with over 100 horses if you're gone?"

"Let me think about it, Joyce. I don't want you to be stressed if anything happens to me."

For about six weeks, the relationship between Ava and Miami had been silent. She kept leaving voice mail on his home machine, and several messages through the receptionist at his office.

He didn't answer but suspected that she wanted to explain.

They both belonged to the same health club, but he knew she could only work out after work and on weekends, so he played basketball on weekday mornings to avoid seeing her. The facts were that the relationship was only a few months old, and they had never said they were exclusive... but to him it had been exclusive...because after meeting her, he didn't want to see anyone else.

Miami re-focused on his work; he was now calling on banks to learn about and purchase foreclosure properties. He had two big offers in on large buildings already and felt like he was turning a corner. He thought, Perhaps I won't have to be lonely and broke. So, he decided to call her and act like nothing had happened. If she was involved with someone else, what could he do? Hell, it would be better to know if she was involved, and then move on, rather than just keep avoiding her. He knew he had never met a woman like Ava and didn't want to shut her out of his life. He wasn't ready to give up on the date they'd made before his trip to Las Vegas and her trip to San Francisco.

Their date was to watch Winning Colors run in the Santa Anita Derby. He decided to see if she still wanted to go to Santa Anita, and called her, agreeing to meet at Starbucks for coffee after work Wednesday.

He got there first, sat at a table, and waited for her entrance. She was wearing jeans with tennis shoes, and looked tired and thin. Her eyes were red. He didn't get up to greet her.

She looked up at him and said, "Mark...I've been trying to talk with you for weeks. I'm so sorry for what happened, and the way it looks... it's not that way...."

"Ava, we never agreed we were exclusive. You...we...."

"No...wait," Ava interrupted him. Her eyes welled up with tears. She seemed to be having trouble getting a full breath. "I'm not seeing anyone. That night...I'm so sorry. I ran into an old boyfriend, I used to work with...and you were in Las Vegas having fun.... It just happened."

She looked down and said, "I broke it off that morning right after you called. I don't care about him. I care about you."

"I could see that…."

Ava reached out and touched his face. He pulled back and looked at her. She folded her hands in her lap. "I'd like to keep trying. You're a different kind of man. I've never been with someone who is as much fun as you. Or, who has as much fun as you. Somehow…you just live…and find adventure. I want to be with you. Just you. Part of that. Please." She leaned forward in her chair, with her arms crossed on the table, and kissed him.

"Ava, I could try to be cool…but…I've missed you. You make me want more out of my life. Yeah, I love the track…and hanging with Dino…but hell, I'm going to be 32. I want a bigger life than that. I just thought we could be…were…something new. Bigger. But if you want to just have…."

She stood up, took a few steps, and sat in his lap, putting her head on his neck.

After a minute, he pulled her head up. "Remember? We were going to go see Winning Colors race and beat the boys in the Santa Anita Derby. Let's just see how it goes…OK? I'll pick you up Saturday morning at 10:00."

April 9, 1988, Santa Anita Racetrack, California

If Winning Colors were to have the opportunity to run in the Kentucky Derby, she would first have to prove herself in today's Santa Anita Derby. She was to run against the best colts in California, at the distance of one-and-one-eighth miles, farther than she had ever run in a race. She always ran so fast early in her races that many top newspaper horse handicappers still believed she could not carry that blinding speed for the longer distances against males.

The day was clear and warm, the track packed with fans, and the ladies in attendance were especially passionate about the filly's chances. Miami noticed the stands were packed with an unusually large number of women, and even young girls. The *Los Angeles Times*, and other local papers, were featuring the race as something of a re-match of the male vs. female tennis game played by Billie Jean King against Bobby Riggs.

Dino told Miami, "Bobby Riggs was an old man at age 55 in that match. Billie Jean King was age 29. This is different, Winning Colors has to beat the best males in California straight up."

Miami and Dino invited Amalia also to see the race, and they left early, knowing the track would be overflowing today. Miami drove the Impala with Ava sitting in the front; Dino and Amalia were in the back seats. Ava surprised all of them with gifts: four blue baseball hats, embroidered with "Winning Colors" in yellow letters. They all donned the hats and smiled.

Miami was being quiet, a rare behavior for him.

Dino explained to Amalia how history proved it would be difficult for their favorite filly to win today. "Horseracing is the only sport in the world where females can compete and win against the men for a championship. How many female horses have won the Santa Anita Derby and then the Kentucky Derby?"

Amalia knew the answer, but she had another question. "None... ever. How have the girls done when racing against the Derby males?"

Dino answered, "Since 1875, only two fillies have won the Derby. And there was one other time...."

Miami looked at Dino in the rear-view mirror...and frowned. Dino was shaking his head side to side.

Ava jumped in, "Tell us. What are you not telling us?"

Dino continued, "It's the worst horse racing story ever. I don't like to think about it or tell it...but, in 1975, there was the greatest filly of all time. Her name was Ruffian, and she was a lot like Winning Colors, with blazing early speed. Ruffian was undefeated in 10 starts with 10 wins. No other filly ever got her head in front of Ruffian ever. All the fans wanted her to run in the Derby, but her trainer and owner said 'no.'"

"She broke the track record in a workout, when she was only 2-years-old!" added Miami.

"So what happened?" asked Amalia. "Tell us."

"So after the Derby they set up a match race. Just her against the 3-year-old colt that won the Derby that year, Foolish Pleasure. They called it 'The Battle of the Sexes' and ran it in New York. It was a huge event, with 50,000 people in attendance and like 18 million watching on TV. Ruffian broke in front and was beating him for three-quarters-of-a-mile."

...

Dino stopped. Tears came into his eyes. He couldn't continue.

Everyone was silent. After thirty seconds, Miami finished the story. "She snapped her front leg in half…but she refused to stop running… she kept trying to beat him and they had to put her down."

There was silence for the rest of the drive to the track.

"Well I can tell you one thing for sure," Dino said. "I have never seen this many women and girls at the racetrack in my entire life. It's because of our girl…they love her."

Many girls and their mothers had posted painted banners and now held pink signs that read: "GIRL POWER!" and "BEAT the BOYS!" Dino and Miami saw the saddling area and paddock packed five persons deep. They were calling out to Winning Colors. She had clearly struck a nerve.

The huge gray filly was wearing the number five saddlecloth and her regular white bridle as she was led to the gate by the saddle pony. Several of the other jockeys were aware of the talents of the big gray filly and had learned of her penchant for getting easily upset. As she warmed up, Stevens noticed that they were using their whips, loudly snapping them against their colts and even their own boots to try to scare her. Stevens was angry about their behavior and steered his mount as far away as possible from the agitators, fearing she could lose her focus before the race even began.

Winning Colors paused and held her head still, as if to take in the beautiful day, with the San Gabriel Mountains standing out against the backstretch. She stood calmly in the gate, waited for the eight males to load, and when the gates snapped open, she promptly raced ahead of the entire field, going straight to the lead. She was immediately challenged to her right and forced to accelerate into the first left turn to hold the lead, while skimming the rail in her usual fashion. This leading group of horses set very fast internal fractions for the distance as the filly exited the first turn, well in front. Stevens was aglow in his bright yellow silks and cap.

Lukas had another top colt also entered in the race named Tejano, ridden by elite jockey Laffit Pincay. It was Tejano and Pincay who took up the bid for the early lead, three paths outside of her.

"They are going quickly out front!" called the race announcer.

The difference in top-class horses verses average thoroughbreds is the ability to go faster early in the race and still persevere in the later stages of the race, when the lower-class horses cannot, or are unwilling, to fight on while nearing exhaustion. Jockey Bill Shoemaker rode the morning line betting favorite horse, Lively One. Seconds into the race, Shoemaker knew the leaders were going way too fast for the distance. He let Lively One wait over seven lengths back, saving energy for the stretch run.

From their vantage point, Dino and Miami waited to see the first two fractions be posted on the infield tote board as an indicator of the suicidal pace these animals were setting, and when it came up in the sprinters time of 22-and-one-fifth, and 45-and-three-fifths seconds, they were worried the colts were pushing Winning Colors too hard. She and the other leaders were bound to tire after this insane speed exhibition. After three-quarters-of-a-mile, she had run in 109-and-two-fifths seconds, it was obvious she was going way too fast and could not be rated to run the full Santa Anita Derby distance.

Stevens let her continue to accelerate, now opening further on the field by three lengths, and then he did something interesting. He bent his head down and took a peek under his right arm to see how far ahead he was, as if he was in control of her. She was not being headstrong and running away with him like some crazy filly! She was setting this fast pace easily. It was as if only she, unlike the others, could run at this incredible pace within herself. The big gray Amazon filly could simply run faster immediately out of the gate than other top stakes class horses could, and Stevens let her have her way.

Winning Colors had distanced herself further from the colts that were chasing her.

As she entered the final left-hand stretch turn, she began to outrun the field, now opening by five lengths, as the fans cheered the lone female in the race. This kind of dominance just doesn't happen in a Grade 1, $500,000 race. Women and girls were standing and yelling, screaming, for the filly to "Beat the boys!"

Shoemaker could see she was stealing away from the field. He ceased reserving Lively One and moved into action on his mount, urging her forward with his arms while chirping to her to move now with an energetic charge against the lightning-bolt-like filly.

Winning Colors took the turns in a more efficient way than the boys; it was as if she was nimbler and more athletic than they were. Something had to give, and it was the colts. Winning Colors was cruising on the lead, still opening further on the field, turning for home now leading by an eye popping seven open lengths!

"Can she hold on? She has to be exhausted!" Dino yelled as Stevens took out his whip and gave her just one left-handed crack on her left flank as she ran full out, practically touching the rail on her left shoulder and appearing to scrape the inner fence. Tens of thousands of women and girl fans were calling out to her along with Dino, Miami, Amalia, and Ava standing and now screaming with them as she raced towards the finish line.

The jockeys on the eight colts were whipping, yelling, and urging on their mounts but could make up no ground as they raced behind the filly. She re-engaged and pulled away even farther from her competitors. Shoemaker now knew he was running for second money at best on Lively One.

Track announcer Trevor Denman reported this exhibition of winning speed in his impeccable English with a South African accent: "Winning Colors is turning in an outstanding performance! We are looking at one exceptional filly that will be carrying the hopes of California all the way to the Kentucky Derby." And then, when she crossed the finish line, "What a winner that one was! Winning Colors! Magnificent!"

Winning Colors had beaten the top California male Kentucky Derby prospects, and she had embarrassed them by seven-and-a-half lengths in exceptionally fast time of 1:47.4 seconds.

Dino and Miami were kissing Amalia and Ava in between high-fiving everyone they could reach while yelling, "We're going to Kentucky! We're going to Kentucky! We're going to Kentucky, baby!"

In the clamor, people at the surrounding tables were asking them, "How much did you bet on her?"

Dino and Miami smiled and looked at each other and said in unison, "We bet her in to win the Kentucky Derby at 50-1!"

That evening, the foursome went to dinner at Chasen's. Miami ordered a bottle of champagne and they all raised a toast to the prospect of Winning Colors winning the Kentucky Derby.

While Dino and Miami talked about the races, Amalia wanted to know about Ava's international travel, and Ava was interested in Amalia's family story of how she had come from Mexico to Beverly Hills. Amalia whispered, "Ava, do you mind that Miami…Mark…is always at the track?"

"What's at the track? Men gambling with other men…and horses… he's done every day by like five p.m. It keeps him out of my hair."

"What about their gambling?"

"They live! Who wakes in the morning happier than these two guys? Doesn't seem to be a problem…they live in nice places…they seem to do well. I know plenty of rich guys that aren't nice…or fun to be with. Mark makes me laugh."

"Dino is like a genius at the track, I hear," Amalia said. "He's hardly a wild gambler. They are both a couple of characters!"

Feelings of celebration were ebbing as Miami and Dino discussed the immediate future. Before her breathtaking win against the colts, the idea of Winning Colors qualifying for the most famous horse race in the world had been an exciting dream. Now it was a certainty, but only if she stayed healthy. The enormity of the moment when the extraordinary gray filly would enter the gate at Churchill Downs weighed on their minds.

Horses are fragile, and they had seen horses favored to win national races catch fevers or sustain minor injuries even on the day of a big race, causing the animal and rider to be scratched. Dino and Miami were nervous, excited, and apprehensive about the necessity of a trip back to Mexico to collect a winning bet. They were talking about their "chance of a lifetime."

Miami half-joked, "Dino, I need you to drive to Santa Anita and put a blanket on her tonight."

Their biggest debate was what her odds would be in the full Derby field. They estimated there would be 16 to 20 horses, which is a huge obstacle. In a large field, the potential to run into horse traffic increases.

An average thoroughbred race has a field of seven to nine horses, but that number is doubled for the Derby. In fact, if there are over 14 entrants, two starting gates are required to be placed side by side, just to accommodate that many animals. The post position, assigned by random draw, is so important that owners and trainers feel a lot of stress just prior. They hope not to draw any of the first five posts for fear of being trapped on the inside. Any mishap, especially at the break, would leave the difficult task of weaving through as many as 19 other horses that hope not to be blocked even once. Many a potential Derby champion lost their best chance at glory just seconds into the race by a poor break onto the track.

The other fear at the post position random draw is getting a gate too far outside. Physics of these outside post positions cause the horses to run wide over the entire race distance of one-and-one-quarter miles. Over 40 percent of the racing is done while in the two turns. Going wide for much of the race makes those outside post horses cover considerably more ground than those horses that get an inside trip.

Because of her ability to achieve early speed, Winning Colors had a huge advantage in such a large field. If she broke well, she should be able to flee the field behind her and let them try to maneuver a successful trip while weaving their way through traffic. In fact, this was the fear of the other trainers; the huge gray filly would break on top and they might never catch her.

Dino said, "I bet she goes off as the 3-1 favorite."

"No, Dino, I think these sexist, male, old timer horse players will bring wheelbarrows full of money to bet against her. Remember? The manager at Agua Caliente told us, 'She cannot win.' I bet the bastard loses his job when he has to pay us!"

"Yes, but women will come out to the track to bet on Winning Colors with both hands!"

The good thing for Miami, Dino, and their fellow big cash gambler at Agua Caliente Big Bernie, was their Mexico future book odds of 50-1 were locked in at that set number. They simply didn't care what race day odds the Churchill Downs fans bet Winning Colors down to, as their Agua Caliente future bets were set at $5,000 to win $250,000 for Dino and Miami, and Big Bernie's $20,000 to win $1,000,000...American dollars...in Mexico.

By comparison, because Luis and his stable friends had wagered one month earlier, before she had won her first stakes race around two turns, their Las Vegas odds were 100-1 on their $2,000 wager to win $200,000.

The other lively debate between Miami and Dino was how to collect the money from the bet they placed at Agua Caliente. This was now a deadly serious topic and several concerns topped their list. Would the race book go out of business if she won? It was rumored the track was in escalating financial trouble now that live racing had ceased. There was no way to understand the corporate legal structure of a Mexican racetrack or the track's true financial health. And then came questions about its owner's ties to the drug cartel's money.

Dino was willing to embrace another chance. "I think we should go down and bet more on her. Seriously."

Miami resisted. "I agree it's a great bet," he said to his friend, "but we have so much risk already, with fear of not getting paid, or even more likely, getting robbed or killed. I'm out."

There was no way for Miami or Dino to presume the amount wagered on Winning Colors at the Agua Caliente future book already, at average odds of nearly 50-1. They guesstimated that $200,000 had been wagered on her, so the track's exposure was likely $10,000,000 or more. That was a lot of money for a financially starved Mexican racetrack.

They discussed the possibility of being robbed after they collected the money. They verified that there was no other option of collecting than being there in person with any winning ticket worth over $1,000. Nor could they get a check. Gamblers dealt in cash. Tax issues also became a concern. Dino felt strongly that they must be at Agua Caliente when Winning Colors won because perhaps only the first persons in line would get paid before there was the equivalent of a run on the bank.

Miami responded by saying, "I'll check on prices for chartering a Brinks armored truck."

"Miami, no way Mexico will allow armed US private guards to take a truck over the border."

The idea of chartering a Mexican armored truck did not instill confidence in the two gamblers either. Miami said, "That's like paying someone to come and rob you."

Dino and Miami were optimistic about the outcome of the race, but now they were frightened, too. Miami came up with an idea: "If we are scared about collecting our $250,000, what about Big Bernie? He's got $20,000 on her at 50-1, according to Twenty Percent Tim. That's $1,000,000 for Christ's sake. I would be scared to death to take $1,000,000 at Santa Anita from the cashier's window to my car. But in fucking Tijuana! He must have a plan. I'll find out tomorrow."

Miami and Dino turned back to Amalia and Ava who were chatting together. The two women were becoming good friends despite coming from different backgrounds. Ava used her hands, gesturing frequently in speaking, while Amalia sat rock still with perfect straight posture and her hands always at her sides or in her lap.

Miami suggested desserts of chocolate soufflé and the girls smiled in approval. After the bottle of champagne, another of chardonnay, and stuffed from two shared desserts, Miami and Dino paid the check.

Dino commented, "If Winning Colors wins the Derby we can almost afford to pay for this dinner."

April 10, 1988, Santa Anita Racetrack, California

At the track on the next day, a Sunday, it didn't take long for Miami to find Big Bernie in the lower clubhouse, alone, eating a carved corned beef sandwich covered in mayonnaise and drinking a Diet Coke, at a stand-up table under a track TV monitor. Forty-one-year-old Big Bernie was wearing a white silk shirt that was way too big for him. A tall man, at six-foot-four, Big Bernie also had a big personality. He wasn't bad looking despite his girth; he was just huge, even while standing next to another big guy like Miami.

Big Bernie's face lit up when he saw his friend. He gave Miami a man hug that nearly crushed the breath out of him. "Miami, my man! You need a loan? Need some help picking a winner? Where's your girlfriend... Dino?" Big Bernie's laugh at his own joke boomed through the clubhouse.

"No Bernie, I don't need a loan. We are going to win our future book bets on Winning Colors."

Big Bernie suddenly got quiet and looked Miami in the eye. "Who told you? Shit, it was Twenty Percent Tim. I knew it. That scumbag."

"He didn't tell me. I figured it out. Look, big guy, it wasn't hard. Which regular track guy do we know who: A) recently had a big score at the betting windows and B) has the balls to bet 20 large on anything? Everyone knows you hit for $200,000 on that Hollywood Park Pick 6…and, Big Bernie…everything about you…is, well…big. I figured it out pretty easy."

Miami opened up to Big Bernie. "We have 5K on her at Agua Caliente. We bet it before she lost to Goodbye Halo, and we got down on her at 50-1. That's $250,000 to us if she hits. It's not shit compared to what you got riding on her, big guy. But…there are some problems about cashing out in Mexico. Like will they pay us or not?"

Big Bernie lowered his voice and said, "I don't want to talk about it here. Take me out to dinner and I'll tell you my plan to get paid. And, bring a nice girl for me, Miami. You know all the ladies, man."

"Meet me at the Warehouse Restaurant in Marina del Rey on Monday night at 8:00 p.m.," was Miami's reply.

Miami picked the Warehouse Restaurant in Marina del Rey because it had a great view of the boats, was 15 minutes from Hollywood Park racetrack, and even more because they served the strongest rum drinks on the planet. He didn't know exactly how many drinks it would take to get a guy the size of Big Bernie loaded, but this place knew how to make a damn good mai tai for sure.

When Miami got there, the song by Kenny Loggins, "Footloose," was being piped into the speakers over the fake bridge, over the fake moat that led to the restaurant that was designed to look like a tropical paradise. Big Bernie was already sitting at the bar with a mai tai in hand, wearing a yellow sports coat and green tennis shoes. Big Bernie gave Miami another crushing bear hug. He signaled the bartender and said, "Get me another mai tai and one for my friend here, too."

"Miami, where do you buy your clothes, man? You look like a big version of Don Johnson! Man, we got to do this more often dude. This is fun! Where are the girls?"

"We'll worry about the girls later."

Bernie looked disappointed, but for two hours they talked while eating sizzling pu pu platters of pork ribs and steak and fish dishes, with their glasses of ice, rum, and fruit juices always full.

"The big score on the $200,000 Pick 6 I hit really did change my life, and not just the money. Man, it made me be ahead of the track and the gambling game for my lifetime. The day I cashed that ticket was the best day in my life. It's just so hard to get a big score like that home. It's not like building a house brick by brick until you're done. It's more like...like a game of Jenga. The thing is so fragile and just when you're almost going to cash it some damn thing can happen and it all falls, like your horse losses by a photo finish, or breaks bad. But the next week after my score, I was sad because I seriously thought about cashing out and quitting the game I love. I love the track like you do, Miami. I'm the happiest when I'm at the track. But it's such a brutally tough game to win at. The house take is like 20 percent and it just grinds you down. The house gets like three or four times what the sports books take out in commission on betting sports."

Big Bernie took a huge draw of his mai tai.

"But Miami, on the other hand, the gamblers at the track are mostly idiots. Like how can I not beat their sorry asses? Most of them have never opened the racing form in their lives. I just have to be a 20 percent better gambler than those idiots who are betting their mom's birthday numbers, or on horses that have pretty names. I study the form, and I know the trainers and their angles. I subscribe to the best insider workout reports on the 2-year-olds in training, so I know how fast those young horses are before anyone else does. I know which post positions are like death for which horses, and which ones are a plus at every distance."

"Are you betting a lot more now since your score?"

"No. I'm betting less most days than before my score, because I know I have capital now to make big bets when I see something I like at good odds. I'm making fewer small bets and more big bets. Miami, I swear I'm not going to give this money back easy. Hey, tell me a track story of your own."

Miami was feeling pretty lit after three drinks.

"OK. Back on July 7, 1977, that's 7-7-77. Right? I'm at the track. The first race comes in...sure enough the number seven horse wins. The second race comes in. Yep, the number seven horse again. So we have a seven-seven daily double. The place is going crazy. We are all waiting for the seventh race of course."

"So what happens in the seventh race?"

"The number seven horse is like 20-1 on the morning line, but the fans hammer him at the windows, betting him down to like the 2-1 favorite!"

"What happens?"

"Sure enough Bernie...he comes in seventh!"

The two men belly laughed for several minutes until Miami steered the conversation back to the Derby. "What do you know about the financial health of Agua Caliente? I hear they are going to go bankrupt. How can they pay us if they're frickin' broke? I'm also hearing some scary things about the owner of the track...that he is mixed up with the cartel down there. I am worried they'll have us robbed or killed on the way from the track to the US border. If you hit your $1,000,000 on Winning Colors, how in the hell are you going to get that kind of serious money back into the country? And, Big Bernie, what about taxes?"

Big Bernie smiled. "That's just it, Miami. I'm not bringing the money back."

Miami looked at him like he was drunk—which he was. "What the hell are you talking about?"

Big Bernie leaned forward, his eyes got wide, and for a moment, Miami thought he was about to cry. "Miami," he said, "you have always been a good friend to me. You treat me good, just like you treat everyone else. But look at me. I weigh almost 400 pounds. What jobs do I get in Los Angeles? Just phone sales jobs, selling loans, or bathroom appliances, or crap. Funny thing is I'm great at it, I'm always the top sales guy everywhere I've gone."

"Man, that sucks."

"I hate it. I don't get girls. I'm just the fat guy." He stopped talking and sat back in the dark booth. Miami could see he was about done talking for the evening, but somehow...it seemed as if he still wanted to tell him more.

"Big Bernie, man, I'm with you, I want to win on this filly, too. I'm worried about you, and about Dino, and about myself, too."

Big Bernie paused. Then he sat up, leaned forward, and said, "Here's my deal. I know a guy who works at the track's race book. I trust him…I think. If Winning Colors wins, I'm going to put my money into the Agua Caliente race book betting account. They take really big bets there. Bigger than Vegas. I won't leave the track with the money, at least for a few weeks, or two months tops. I figure they won't kill me if I deposit the money with them. Shit…they probably figure I'll just lose it back. Then I'll have my Mexican attorney transfer the money to his legal trust account, or a Mexican real estate escrow account. Miami, I won't lose it back! I'm going to buy a motel on the beach in Rosarito, 10 miles south of Tijuana. I've already picked it out. It's so beautiful! You will love it. You and Dino can come down and party with me on the beach. Bring some girls. It's like a one-hour drive south of the Del Mar racetrack."

Big Bernie was smiling and open. His beefy arms were wide open, and he held his palms up. "Miami, if our filly wins the Derby, man I'm staying in Mexico. I'll own my own motel right on the beach, and I'll never have to work again. I'll be known as '*el jefe* Bernie.' No, I'll be Don Bernie, you know, like in the *Godfather* movie…Don Corleone."

By now, Miami was exhausted. He called a cab to get them both home. He didn't want to say anything that would ruin Big Bernie's dream. He now wanted Winning Colors to just stay healthy, and get into that Derby starting gate, not just for him and Dino, but even more for Big Bernie.

CHAPTER 8

Newspaper Execution

The morning of Wednesday, April 20, 1988, was cold and raining in Tijuana, Mexico. Hector Felix Miranda, known by his famous *Zeta* newspaper pen name, El Gato, awoke to get ready for his workday. In this city of great poverty, and great wealth, the bachelor El Gato followed an unwavering schedule. He woke, dressed, and had breakfast at the same café every morning. Often, he met with people during breakfast to learn new content for the gossip and news column he wrote, but his favorite subject was always Jorge Rhon.

As he got dressed, El Gato did not notice it, but he was being watched through binoculars. He also did not notice the black Trans Am sports car that was parked across the steep street. He donned his Members Only gray jacket, grabbed his colorful umbrella, walked to his Crown Victoria sedan, then paused to speak to his young neighbor, Ejival, a student at Universidad Iberoamericana.

El Gato warmed up the engine and turned on the windshield wipers before he drove down the narrow Tijuana street. It was 9:00 a.m. and the short drive was the last thing this journalist ever did.

Victoriano Medina Moreno, the man with the binoculars, whispered, "The target is on the move," over a two-way radio and receiver to his accomplice, Antonio Vera Palestina, who was waiting in ambush mode, a ways down the street. The streets were wet, filled with potholes, and El Gato's huge car was moving slow. A third accomplice, Emigdio Nevárez, moved his pick-up truck into a position that blocked El Gato's car. Palestina exited the truck and pointed a high-powered shotgun at El Gato. The first bullets ripped El Gato's shoulder and neck to pieces. The murderer and his accomplice moved to a point six feet away to shoot El Gato from behind the wheel of his car. The second blast hurled his dead body into the passenger seat and separated much of his head from his torso. The Crown Victoria kept moving downhill before crashing into a house.

A journalist was dead. A message had been sent.

The drivers of the pick-up truck and the Trans Am departed the scene in separate directions. Ten minutes later, they met again at the Agua Caliente racetrack parking lot. The drivers clocked in to work at their jobs in the security office of the racetrack.

The next night, Dino's telephone rang at 11:00 p.m. and the sound woke him. "What's up?" he answered. "It's late."

It was Amalia. "You have me always checking on that Tijuana newspaper, *Zeta*...right?...and you said you wanted to know about anything El Gato, that Mexican reporter, who writes about the track and its owner...right?"

"Yeah, of course, of course, thanks...what...?"

"Well, *Zeta* released today a special edition. El Gato was shot to death, execution style, in broad daylight."

"Whoa, whoa...are you sure?" As Dino sat up in bed, he said, "That's the reporter who was writing the bad shit about Jorge Rhon, the track owner, right?"

"Yes, I'm sure. I got a call from a friend of mine who is a librarian down in San Diego. She's been reading the papers to me when she finds stuff on him. It's the biggest story in years in Tijuana."

"What else do you know? Do they have a suspect?"

"That's it so far, but I'll call you when I get to work tomorrow and get everything else I can find out," said Amalia and she hung up.

Dino knew Miami was always up late, so he called and told him the story.

"Shit, Dino! That's awful about the journalist...and as for Rhon... well, he can't pay us if he's in jail."

Neither Miami nor Dino slept well the rest of that night.

They both went to see Amalia at the end of day on Saturday, at the library. She wore a grave expression and had much more information to share. "Apparently there is a lot of wealth there, mostly by the politicians and the cartels. I don't really know, but they have big beauty pageants, and championship boxing matches, and big weddings and stuff...."

"So, here's what we know now," said Amalia. "El Gato used to be friends with the owner of the track, Rhon, and went to his events and hung out with him. For many years, he wrote about him, and it wasn't too bad. El Gato sometimes criticized Rhon for being an outsider; the native Tijuanans hated guys that came from Mexico City, but El Gato liked Rhon because Rhon loved Tijuana, and loved his house, his track. Rhon became one of the prominent locals. El Gato also made fun of everyone and wasn't afraid to call out the mayor, or anyone. Their paper, *Zeta*, is respected and not afraid of calling out the drug cartels, the corruption, and the politicos. El Gato wrote about torture."

"Holy shit," said Miami. "These *Zeta* newspaper guys are brave dudes. So how is Rhon tied to this at all?"

"People think that Rhon ordered the hit on El Gato, because El Gato was very critical of Rhon. That's why they also assumed that Rhon ordered his men to use Uzi machine guns on the front of the *Zeta* newspaper offices last month—to send a message to El Gato and *Zeta* to back off...'or else'...and I guess this is the 'or else' part. But here is what's important—guess who they are looking for in the murder of El Gato?"

"Who?" Dino asked.

She grabbed the necklace on her throat, "Rhon's bodyguard, Antonio Vera Palestina. He works as the head of security for the Agua Caliente racetrack! The guy is missing, along with another track security guard named Moreno."

The library became even quieter as the three of them tried to process the information. Amalia's source in San Diego also said that over a dozen journalists had been killed in Mexico over the last six years.

"These guys kill people for just saying bad things about them," said Miami. "What do they do to the people who win millions?"

In the days after they received news of El Gato's murder, the discussions between Dino and Miami became heated on the topic of where to watch the Kentucky Derby. Miami wanted to go to Kentucky to have some fun and party.

"Don't you think that that may be just a wee bit premature?" Dino asked. "She still hasn't won the Derby, there are like 16 other talented colts that can beat her, and we have the owner of the race book in Mexico having security guards kill people. Look, he's not going to kill or rob people on the day of the Kentucky Derby, right? Agua Caliente will be packed that day. Even the parking lots will be full. And there will be a ton of other bettors there that bet on her too, mostly on like small $50 tickets. I say we go in person that day and bring a container to carry our money home when she wins."

"Dino?"

"What?"

"How big a container do you need to carry $250,000 in cash?"

"How the hell would I know?" said Dino. "Will they pay us in hundreds or twenties? OK. Let's figure for both. It might be 2,500 bills in hundreds or 12,500 bills in twenties. I figure that's about three to four of those giant black trash bags, you know the big ones, if they pay us in twenties."

This image was hilarious to the two gamblers and it took several minutes before they could recover from laughing.

"OK, let me get this right," said Miami. "You want us to drive across the Mexican border, go into the Agua Caliente racetrack carrying giant plastic lawn trash bags, watch the race on TV...and...when she wins the Derby...we go up to the window, where they will count out 12,500 twenty-dollar bills. We then just pack 'em up and casually stroll to my indiscreet red sports car...because I'm not driving your slow-as-hell Impala...to pick up $250,000 in cash."

"We could take a cab, I guess."

Again, several minutes of laughter.

"All kidding aside, I think we have to take my car," said Miami. "Remember? I used to race. I swear to God if you get me in my 300Z they won't catch me until we hit the border! And if we get to the border they aren't going to kill us in front of the US Border Patrol guards, right?"

"You can outrun a bullet? Does your car even have a trunk?"

"Not really a trunk...so suitcases are probably out. OK, we are back to the trash bag idea. God, just let our sweet filly win!"

Sunday, May 1, 1988, was a sunny, beautiful, 80-degree Los Angeles spring day. With just six days to the Derby, Dino and Miami made the 40-minute drive from West Los Angeles to Santa Anita. This racetrack is far prettier in the winter months when there is virtually no smog, and the mountains with snow-capped peaks are visible, giving a beautiful backdrop to the track. In summer months, smog can be prevalent on hot days and the mountains become barely visible. Dino and Miami were soon seated at their regular table in the turf club, and their excitement level was even higher than normal.

In addition to their worries that the prime execution killing murder suspect was now the owner of the racetrack, Dino had a new problem on his mind. "Miami, I've been handicapping the field of Derby horses our girl will face in the race next week. Unfortunately, it is by far the toughest field I've seen in years. Just listen to the competition Winning Colors is up against." He read the information and inserted commentary.

"Risen Star, winner of six races already, including the Louisiana Derby and the Kentucky Derby prep last month, and a son of Secretariat.

"Next, Private Terms. This horse is frickin' undefeated! Seven starts and seven wins! This horse could go off as the favorite. He just won the Gotham and the Wood Memorial. Raced against the best and has never been beaten! Private Terms' grandfather is Secretariat.   "Now, Seeking the Gold. He almost beat undefeated Private Terms' last race in the Gotham Stakes.

"Forty Niner. This horse is a beast. Winner of six stakes already, just lost to Risen Star by a head, and trained by Woody Stephens. Ah, Woody Stephens. I hate that guy; he never shuts up. Forty Niner has good speed and can sit just off Winning Colors and try to out finish us. He scares the hell out of me! This horse was the champion 2-year-old in the country last year, winning two Grade 1 stakes at Saratoga by seven total lengths. This horse has been the future book favorite for like over a year now."

Miami asked Dino to stop.

Dino shook his head and said, "Miami, we really, I mean she really, has gotten unlucky to have to run in the Derby this year against such an awesome field of colts. In any normal year she would be the odds-on favorite to win, but this year she may not even be the favorite."

"Yeah, but everyone thinks she is just some little filly that will get smoked by the boys. I've been reading too, and she is now over 1,200 pounds of legs and muscle. She is by far the biggest and tallest horse in the race. These colts won't know what hit them when she breaks out of the gate and goes right to the front!"

The 1988 race was the most anticipated Kentucky Derby since Secretariat won in 1973. Everyone had a different opinion of who would win this stellar edition of the world's most famous horse race. Woody Stephens was mouthing off about his 2-year-old champion Forty Niner. Many knowledgeable horse people were saying that the field had a real problem on their hands with Winning Colors in the race, as she gave the field a perhaps insurmountable problem. If the field let her have her way on the lead uncontested, she could then slow the pace of the race down, and save her energy for the stretch, and they likely could not catch her. But to send a horse to run with the gray Amazon early was considered suicide because she ran at such an insane high cruising speed, the other horse would get fried trying to run with her at the start and would fall apart in the long Churchill Downs track home stretch.

Woody Stephens said of Winning Colors on the lead: "She's not gonna get loose, don't worry about it. If I turn her loose, I might as well go on home."

As was usual for the Kentucky Derby field of 3-year-old horses, no horse had yet been asked to run the one-and-one-quarter-mile distance. Risen Star had just won the Lexington Stakes, the Kentucky Derby prep race two weeks earlier, and had sat back in last place for the early part of that race, before he swept to a neck and neck victory over Forty Niner. Risen Star stayed back as many as 14 lengths behind fast early pace runners, saving energy for one tremendous run to victory in the stretch.

In an interview about Winning Colors before the Derby, Lukas stated, "This field can hit her from every angle, but I don't think they will be able to run with her early, and hopefully the big field in the Derby will cause traffic trouble for many of the closers like Risen Star. The last eighth of a mile will be the test for her, but I believe in my heart she is the best and will win this race."

Dino and Miami were also worried about Goodbye Halo entering the Kentucky Derby field. Her trainer had recently paid a $3,000 late nominating fee to keep her eligible for the Triple Crown honor, which is winning the Kentucky Derby, Preakness Stakes, and the Belmont Stakes. They were thrilled to hear Goodbye Halo's trainer quoted earlier in the week saying, "There's too much money to be made just by running within her own division. And I think Mr. Hancock would love to win the Kentucky Oaks." The Kentucky Oaks, for 3-year-old fillies, is run at Churchill Downs the day before the Kentucky Derby and is the most prestigious race in the country for 3-year-old fillies.

In their continuing conversations, it was Miami who broached the subject of the assassination of El Gato. "How does Jorge Rhon being suspected of the murder affect us? Apparently, the murderers are his racetrack security guys. What if they arrest Rhon?"

"These politicos are protected in Mexico. His dad was the mayor of Mexico City. I bet nothing ever happens to him. Still, I know the racetrack is in serious financial trouble and this has to hurt big time. Who in the hell is going to go to Agua Caliente racetrack now—with the track's guards in the newspapers every day as murder suspects? Do you want to go make bets there? It doesn't matter that they offer better future book odds than Las Vegas. Everyone will just go to Vegas. That Mexican racetrack is toast. I worry that if Winning Colors wins, they'll just close the doors. Why pay out tens of millions now and then file bankruptcy a few months later?"

"I've been reading that Rhon still has a chance to get Mexico licensed as a sports book betting company. He has to keep that going. It would make a ton of money. If he doesn't pay the Winning Colors bet, then no gambler will ever bet with him again. I think he will pay... and Dino?

You know that's the gamblers' code, man. You may not pay your rent, or your car payment, but you always pay your gambling debts…that's the way it works."

Miami was quiet until he could articulate even more fear. "What I am really concerned about is that after she wins…they'll know we are coming to collect our money. There are bad guys all over and they know a bunch of gringos are coming to collect millions of dollars in cash if she wins. They are probably setting the roadblocks for us now. We have to think this thing through. Jesus Christ, this is scary."

They agreed to meet again later that night to make their plans for watching the race and cashing the biggest score of their gambling lives.

Luis woke at 3:30 a.m. and put on some clean jeans, his better pair of black cowboy boots, a clean white long-sleeved shirt, and his tan cowboy hat. He kissed Mariana goodbye, grabbed his duffel bag, and headed to his pick-up truck. He had a plane to catch with his favorite horse.

When he arrived at the barn at 4:15 a.m., Winning Colors had already been fed and her legs were wrapped. She came to the front of the stall to meet him, or perhaps for the carrots she knew he would bring. He talked to her softly in Spanish, telling her that it would be a long day of travel to Kentucky, but he would stay with her as much as he could. He'd traveled with her before to New York and back, knew she was high strung, and he was worried about anything happening to her before her debut in Kentucky. He hooked up her halter, which she now allowed only Luis to do, and he led her from her stall for the quarter-mile walk to the horse transportation van at the Santa Anita barn entrance.

Their drive to the airport was one hour away. She was calm and still as he walked her up the ramp to the custom-made trailer. The trailer was clean as an operating room and Jeff Lukas already had placed the type of fresh straw and water preferred by the horse on the floor of her tight stall. Another two horses were already on the van across from her and were going to Kentucky as well. Luis rode with her to the airport in the cab of the truck.

The Boeing 727 could fly as many as 21 horses, but today there were just five making the flight. Luis was glad she would not be alone;

she seemed to enjoy the sense of safety being next to other horses gave her, even if she often tried to bite them. If she was the first one on, and first one off the van or the plane, she tended to stay calm. He led her down the ramp into the horse stall that would be then lifted on a special forklift to the tall jet. The padded travel stall was also lined with the Lukas brand of fresh straw and water, but was small and close, designed to keep her in a tight box to avoid her moving and hurting herself if there was air turbulence during the four-hour flight. She did not want to enter the tight box, but he had saved carrots for this reason. Luis went to the front of the stall and when she saw him and the carrots he offered, she moved in with ease.

For liability reasons, Luis could not stay with her during the flight, as only the horse flight crew was allowed. He would be on the same flight, yes, but not with her in the holding stall. He saw the horse stalls being hydraulically lifted into the hold and he left to take his seat. He hated to leave her, even for a few hours.

As the plane took flight, Luis thought about how he drove an old unreliable pick-up truck, but the horses flew in new private jets. He was happy for her and would not have had it any other way.

Six hours later, after the flight and subsequent van ride, Luis led Winning Colors down the van ramp to her temporary stall at the historic Churchill Downs racetrack, in Louisville, Kentucky. Like all new horse arrivals from out of state, she would be quarantined for 48 hours in the barn stall area before being led to the special barn section reserved for the elite Derby contestants.

Miami and Dino met at their favorite Mexican restaurant for happy hour, just west of Santa Anita, and ordered a blended strawberry margarita for Dino and a Cadillac margarita on the rocks with salt, for Miami. They were not in joking moods and got right into a heated debate.

Miami wanted to go to Louisville to watch the race in person. "Hell, even if we lose, we will never in our lifetime have this moment at the Derby again," he said. "Let's ride it out in person and make a week out of it we'll never forget! Come on Dino, it's not a business, it's a horse race!"

Dino waited for Miami to calm down and get some tequila in his bloodstream before responding. "Yes, it's exciting and a chance of a lifetime, but it is a business for me, or at least I want it to be. I can't be spending thousands of dollars partying with you in Kentucky, and then come home empty if she loses. If she wins this year, and we collect, I promise I'll go next year with you. But for now, we need to treat this as a business. So, what's the best way for us to get paid and not get mugged or worse?"

"I agree the safest day to collect is in TJ on Derby day, in person. I've never been to Agua Caliente on Derby day, but for sure it will be packed, and we have to be safer surrounded by thousands of people, right?" Miami sounded like he was still working to convince himself that it would be safe.

"Yes, I know it will be crowded, and we have to go there before we even know if she will be a winner. Damn, we are going to be depressed if she loses and we have to drive home with empty trash bags."

"I'll have to put you on suicide watch if that happens. OK, if we drive down on Derby Saturday, the race won't go off until like 4:00 p.m. our time, and I know we will want to play the other Derby races. The card will be awesome with full horse fields and all that stupid money in the pools from people that bet on their favorite colors and shit. And I have to drive. Obviously, we can't get in a cab with 250K on us!"

"There's another problem. Amalia and I researched the border laws and we are not allowed to bring in more than $10,000 each without declaring it to US Customs."

"Shit…now you tell me. Are we going to declare it? Then we would have to pay taxes! I'm not doing that!"

"I have a plan I'm thinking about. What if we pay say 23 guys to come with the two of us and they each carry back 10K? Or what if we have, say, eight guys, and we make three separate trips?"

"Who knew it was so hard to win a quarter of a million dollars? Now I know why Big Bernie is keeping the money down in Mexico. Can you imagine this discussion if we were talking four times that amount… hell, who are we kidding, that's the greatest problem I ever heard of!"

Miami and Dino had two full plates of arroz con pollo, and steaming carnitas, with two more grande margaritas before coming to agreement to watch the Kentucky Derby live on TV in Mexico, at the track. Dino agreed to bring a suitcase and clothes bags for the cash and Miami would figure out the car insurance. They couldn't agree whether to bring muscle with them in the form of other guys, or just risk the border crossing without declaring the money, but they were too clouded with tequila to complete the plan that evening.

CHAPTER 9

The Greatest Two Minutes

Louisville is horse country and it embraces everything associated with racing, from bourbon to gambling. The city is a throwback to a different, slower time. Think drinking a mint julep on a hot afternoon while watching horses race—it's an art form to be savored and enjoyed.

For one May weekend each year, the jet set arrives a bit early in Louisville to transform the city into a place like Monte Carlo or Beverly Hills. The jets were pouring in as early as Wednesday and professional athletes were ready to party. NBA superstar Julius Erving (aka "Dr. J.") was seen laughing with Jim Kelly, the star quarterback of the Buffalo Bills. Steve Garvey of the Los Angeles Dodgers was present, along with Art Rooney, the legendary owner of the Pittsburgh Steelers. They were wined and dined at the parties leading up to the big race. College basketball coach Bobby Knight of Indiana (famous for throwing a temper tantrum and a chair onto the court during a game in 1985) was friends with Lukas. He told the trainer, "You are so competitive that when you lose the race, you think you are going to win the replay."

The week of the Kentucky Derby is frenetic in Louisville. The town pays respect to its racing history by nicknaming every bar, restaurant, street, and men's room with a word or name related to horseracing. Wealthy locals entertain their transient, affluent guests at gala charity events and fashion shows. The public parties at the annual Great Steamboat Race, between The Belle of Louisville and The Delta Queen, held on the Wednesday before the Derby. Dozens of huge private parties lead up to race day, where movie stars mingle with politicians. The Kentucky Colonels Party draws 500 revelers for the event each year, with racing being secondary to drinking cocktails. The Derby fans' activities and access to the pre-race festivities separates them by income level. Hotel rooms increase prices by over 500 percent.

Most of the Kentucky Derby attendees have no real interest in horseracing, or even gambling, but are there because, like the Super Bowl, it is a world-class party. The charity events are by invitation only, individual seats in the back of the ballroom begin at hundreds of dollars per ticket, and a well-located table of eight can be priced upwards of $10,000.

The richest people attending in 1988 were found at the elite, invitation-only party of Preston and Anita Madden. The Maddens' parties had become legendary. Each year featured a theme. That year's theme was Imperial Russia, featuring giant, Fabergé style eggs. Apparently, the years of Imperial Russia (1600-1900) featured hot women in sexy outfits, as the female attendees spent months preparing for the event and arrived in custom beaded gowns with plunging necklines, or for the younger set, mini dresses that left little to the imagination.

Annie Potts of the TV show *Designing Women* won the prize for hottest outfit of the night for her clinging black miniskirt. Queen of the 1988 event was Zsa Zsa Gabor, who at age 71 looked great in a pink gown, with five pounds of jewelry. The photographers and paparazzi abandoned her when the biggest star of the weekend arrived: Larry Hagman of the TV show *Dallas*. He was sporting a huge cowboy hat. Hollywood people seem to love athletes, and athletes seem to love hanging with the Hollywood people. The wealthy attendees mingled with singer Kenny Rogers, and former Miss Americas, Phyllis George and Mary Ann Mobley, who were there with their husbands.

The stamina a racehorse needs to run the Derby's distance of one-and-one-quarter miles was rivaled by the partiers' abilities to survive the Friday night soirées and still make the Derby the next day. Saturday, many in the same group appeared at the expensive Millionaires Row in the Turf Club of Churchill Downs for catered food and cocktails. The women were focused on their colorful hats instead of gowns and mini dresses. Tickets to the Millionaires Row event were nearly impossible to acquire without inside racing connections.

Derby day in Louisville is a special sporting event because of the gambling, yet the professionals who run most tracks act as if they would be shocked to learn gambling is occurring on the premises. Track professionals never refer to their customers as gamblers, only as race fans. The average fan watching the NBA Finals, or Super Bowl, doesn't really care who wins the game unless their local team is playing. The 150,000 Derby fans in attendance make significant bets for themselves and are fully engaged financially in the spectacle. Any gambler at the Derby will always remember if the horse they chose won.

The first time Miami attended the Kentucky Derby in 1984, he was shocked to see the size of the crowd on the Friday before the Saturday running of the Derby. The Friday feature is always the Kentucky Oaks, the 3-year-old, females-only rendition of the Kentucky Derby. Females could enter against the boys in the Kentucky Derby, but colts were not permitted in the Kentucky Oaks. When Miami attended the Oaks Friday races, he thought he had found paradise—full fields of top horses to wager on, and a party that wouldn't stop. The Oaks Friday party featured a sophisticated crowd, with well-dressed men in sports coats, and many beautiful women dressed in stylish short dresses and heels.

The locals were there to party and could drink mint juleps and other hard liquor in impressive quantities, unlike the Los Angeles crowd he was used to (people who drank only white wine). Miami thought, Wow, if this is what it's like the day before the Derby, what will the Derby be like?

Weather conditions on Derby day can be 40 degrees or 80 degrees, and the race is run even if it is pouring rain. Umbrellas are prohibited; only raincoats are permitted. On race day in 1984 at Churchill Downs, the temperature was 71 and the weather was cloudy. Miami arrived at the Derby in his best sports coat and a monogramed, custom-made shirt. He was disappointed to see a beer-drinking crowd that probably would have been more comfortable at a Cleveland Browns tailgating party, or a WrestleMania event. He learned that all the Kentucky social and professional elite attend only the Friday Kentucky Oaks day each year and leave the insane Kentucky Derby Saturday party to the amateurs. The elite have private parties with huge television screens at their homes.

The average total Derby day attendance at Churchill Downs is around 150,000 fans, with over 80,000 of the attendees in the infield where there is no seating and usually no view of the races at all. Miami noticed that the infield participants were there for partying and drinking, and they were damn good at it.

Entertainment in the infield featured rock bands and mosh pits, but few restrooms. The rest of the racetrack was pleasant to experience that Derby day, despite the crowds, as Churchill Downs learned, in over 100-plus years, how to properly run a huge event.

The track has enough ticket vendors to allow bettors to wager, enough bars for anyone to get a drink, and enough TV screens to watch the odds and races. Days like this were made for knowledgeable handicappers like Dino, Miami, and Big Bernie. The betting pools were huge, and the bettors mostly unsophisticated. The chance for a big score was exciting. Because many of the professional horse gamblers' best days for profits come on the days of big races, Miami and Dino would bet five times as much as they would during the running of an average race card.

Lukas, Klein, and Stevens had met in the late afternoon the week of the 1988 Derby and discussed their plans for handling the negative comments about their female's chances in the race.

Lukas told them, "Let's let them talk all the negative crap they want about her. Let's not let them know what we have in our girl. Maybe… just maybe…they will underestimate her and let us get an uncontested early lead."

Stevens nodded in agreement and said, "The biggest knock I hear from the jockeys is they don't think she can go the one-and-one-quarter mile distance. They think she'll tire and quit."

"Good. Let them think that…because if she gets an easy early lead she will kick their asses!" said Klein.

They all were feeling confident but agreed to just keep quiet.

The family of Gary Stevens had been to his first Kentucky Derby ride in 1985. His dad told him, "I don't ever want to go back…too crowded and uncomfortable."

However, in 1988, Gary told his entire family, "You have to come to this year's race. I'm going to win it."

So, they booked their tickets and hotels.

Jeff Lukas had planned the details of Winning Colors' pre-race day. After a light jog around the track and her usual warm sponge bath, he took the halter away from Luis. Winning Colors was going to have a special treat—a slow walk, so she could graze on fresh grass along the road near the stable area. He thought it would calm and relax her. An accomplished horseman, Lukas kept his hands firmly on her halter lead while she put her head down to graze, happy to be out of her enclosed stall.

What happened next was a surprise.

A motorcycle went by on the road and backfired with a loud pop, just feet from her head. Startled, she bolted away from the frightening noise. Lukas was pulled off his feet by the 1,200-pound animal. He held on for his life as she careened toward the stable that was brimming with trucks, equipment, and other horses. His knees and elbows were torn up and bleeding as she dragged him, but he would not let go, fearing her start in the Derby would end in tragedy before her race. After he got her to pull up, he searched her body with his hands, feeling for a bump, cut, or signs of blood.

Unlike Lukas, she was no worse for the wear. He limped her back to Luis who grabbed her halter. Luis called for help for Jeff then took the horse back to her stall where he further inspected her head to toe, no injuries.

An assistant trainer who had witnessed the frightened horse drag Jeff around like a piece of meat and told other backstretch workers, "It took incredible guts for Jeff to hang on to her. Her Derby and career could have ended this morning."

That night, Luis slept just outside of her stall in case she had any issues during the night.

Dino and Miami had taken great interest in the Friday running of the Grade 1 Kentucky Oaks, because the only horse to have beaten Winning Colors, Goodbye Halo, was the favorite. If Goodbye Halo lost to the top field of fillies, it would reflect negatively on the quality of Winning Colors.

During the Oaks race, they witnessed the exact opposite.

Goodbye Halo had been bet down to odds on, and when the gates opened, she devastated the other runners in the field by three-and-three-quarters lengths. The purse for the female race was only $242,600, compared to the purse for the Kentucky Derby the next day of $786,200. Considering that Winning Colors beat Goodbye Halo by over nine lengths in their last meeting at Santa Anita, it made Dino and Miami even more confident of Winning Colors' talent. They were having trouble concentrating on betting the races that weekend; the chance of winning $250,000 on Winning Colors was their sole focus.

Well, that and staying alive to enjoy the money.

The morning of the Derby saw fans lining up to get in at 6:00 a.m., with the largest attendance of women the track had ever experienced. It's possible that every woman in America was rooting for Winning Colors. Interest in and viewership of this race was way up because of the gray filly.

The Kentucky Derby was the eighth race on the Saturday card, which was fortunate for the revelers from the Friday night parties that ended after two a.m. The TV station NBC had their "A Team" of broadcasters on hand for feature interviews with Eugene and Joyce Klein, Gary Stevens, and D. Wayne Lukas.

Lukas was dressed to perfection in a dark suit, white shirt, and red tie, but acted less brash than normal when he said into the camera, "Given all the things that can happen, and especially the setbacks I've experienced in the Derby, I want to fall head over heels, but I am a little bit guarded. If she wins I'll be won over completely…if she goes to the front on her own easily. Hopefully, we will get a Hollywood ending today."

At approximately five p.m., the trainers and handlers led the Derby horses from the barn to the saddling arena. Many of the owners also made the long walk in the dirt with their horses. The owners knew this event was truly the chance of a lifetime, and they were blessed in a special way to make the historic walk with a talented horse.

Winning Colors was disinterested in the crowd and the noise level but was open to biting other horses when the opportunity presented itself. She pranced around and occasionally darted at the colts. She was calm and steady, with her head held high as Luis led her to the saddling arena. The Derby crowd was so much louder than anything these horses had experienced in their short careers. There is always a risk that the high-strung horses might become so agitated from the commotion they'd waste energy, and not run their best race.

The owners and the trainers know that the single racing question they will always be asked is, "Did you ever win the Derby?" Lukas had entered 12 other horses and had never won, despite winning nearly every other stakes race. Despite his leadership in the national earnings stats, his lack of success in the Derby bothered him.

Woody Stephens, trainer of Forty Niner, also bothered him. Woody was a Hall of Fame trainer and was at an age where he said whatever he wanted, whenever he wanted. He'd said to the press, "Winning Colors does not belong in the Derby and will not win the race."

Lukas would not be bullied and responded to Woody's comment: "I don't expect Forty Niner to be able to handle the Derby distance."

Their dislike of each other was real.

Back in Los Angeles, Miami conceded to Dino and agreed to go to Agua Caliente to watch the race on the Tijuana track's television screens during the Kentucky Derby. If Winning Colors won, they'd cash the bet and get the hell out of Mexico fast and alive. They still couldn't decide if they would declare their winnings at the border. They'd agreed to make the decision last minute on the way from the track back to the US Customs station.

The night before the Derby, Miami made what he thought was a good suggestion to Dino: "Let's take two cars. If one of us gets stopped, we won't lose all the money. Just half."

"No way I'm driving around Tijuana with hundreds of thousands in cash on me in the Hotel Impala. That car is old and not dependable. Even more, I have a terrible sense of direction. I'll never be able to keep up with you and I know you won't wait for me. If I get lost, what am I supposed to do? Stop at a gas station? Are you nuts?"

Miami smiled. "You forgot to mention you drive like your grandmother, too. Can they confiscate my car if we don't claim the cash at the border and get caught? I don't want to lose that car, man. I love her. I've got a lot of history in that baby."

They agreed to take Miami's 300Z because it was faster, and Miami's response was, "What smuggler would be brash enough to smuggle drugs back across the border in a red sports car, for Christ's sake? They'll see a blond California-looking guy driving a convertible and wave us right back into the good old USA!" Still smiling, Miami said, "Dino, I need you to dye your hair blond and learn how to talk like a surfer."

Around eight the next morning, Miami was wearing his usual white, short-sleeved silk jacket when he left to pick up his friend. He found Dino in front of his Santa Monica apartment building holding a big white suitcase. It had a pink handle.

"What the fuck is that? It'll never fit in my trunk."

"It's my mom's. I told her to bring a suitcase and she brought hers, not my dad's. What could I do? It was late last night, and we need one for the money, right?"

The suitcase barely fit into the car.

Now Miami was driving fast and being talkative about the day's adventure. Dino was feeling sick to his stomach.

"Dino! Don't worry, man! Look, two guys drive to a Tijuana racetrack in a red Z to bet on a filly to win the Kentucky Derby against 16 of the best male horses in the country and if she wins they collect 250 grand from suspected Mexican cartel members. Then they drive the money, like a bat out of hell, from the racetrack to an international border, where they don't declare the money. Dino, what could possibly go wrong?"

Miami pulled off at a freeway exit south of San Diego to get some cheeseburgers and purchase car insurance for Mexico. Jimmy, the sales manager, was nervous about the fact that Miami wanted to insure the car for over $200,000.

"OK, Jimmy…say the Mexican federales confiscate my car. Will I be insured? How about if the US Customs guys seize my car and I am found not to have drugs? I want it in writing that if that happens I'm fully covered."

Jimmy asked, "How many days will you be on vacation in Mexico?"

"Like five, maybe six hours."

Insurance policy done and cheeseburgers consumed, Miami and Dino drove south. Dino had a map of Tijuana in his lap.

Their world changed the instant they were waved through the Mexican border. Miami said, "Apparently, few people sneak things into Mexico."

The two gamblers kept driving into roundabouts with cars entering from five different entry streets, and the taxis were playing a game of chicken with all the other cars, and even with the trucks. They saw two near misses in one roundabout. Dino named them, "*circulos de accidentes*." The trucks did not have mufflers, and each one was louder than a thunderstorm. Miami watched the road signs and exits knowing he would soon have to drive back through these streets. He worried about being chased by criminals at the same time, possibly in the dark.

It took 20 minutes to get from the border crossing to the Agua Caliente parking lot. Dino and Miami had planned to do a dry run practice drive from the track back to the border, but the traffic heading north was already too heavy. They scrapped that plan and Miami told Dino, "The hell with that...I need a drink."

"Miami," Dino said, pleading, "take it easy today. I need you at full power, mi amigo."

They entered the race book about 12:30 p.m., still three hours before the Derby post time. Despite Miami's request to leave it in the car, Dino wheeled in the pink handled white suitcase with trash bags stuffed inside.

"Think positive, Miami. No negative waves."

The place was jumping with activity. There were far more horseplayers than when they'd visited four months ago. The betting lines were 20 deep with gamblers making bets on a race 3,000 miles away. Dino studied the racing form then got in line to bet the stakes races offered on the Derby undercard.

Miami had given Dino $200 and told him to bet it for him. While Dino waited at the window, Miami looked for two seats. It was so crowded, he felt lucky just to elbow his way to the bar to order a double Cuba Libre with premium aged Mexican rum. He looked around for Camila, his favorite waitress. She was serving a huge tray of six grande margaritas to a group of boisterous men. He could tell it was not their first round. He also noticed that there were two super-hot girls wearing

Patron Tequila sashes over their tight green mini dresses. Wearing tennis shoes, the girls were serving shots of Patron to the gamblers. The girls allowed customers to lick the salt and lime juice off their skin before taking the tequila shots.

A loud argument broke out in the back of the bar and several beer bottles shattered on the floor. Three rough looking security guards with rifles ran in, got everyone to take a seat, and things calmed down.

An eight-man mariachi band whose members were wearing giant bright red and green straw sombreros, white frilled shirts with red bolo ties, and tight black pants, strolled into the race book while playing Mexican songs on their five guitars and three trumpets. The noise level went from loud to deafening.

Some drunk guy decided to try dancing with Camila as she worked to detach herself from him. The group of guys that had just ordered the six grande margaritas were singing now, and Miami was starting to feel good, too. With the chilled rum in his system, he took a deep breath and relaxed for the first time that day. Miami felt that something about mariachi music made him want to say, "Fuck it! Let's party!" Dino was still standing in line, watching a television monitor before the fifth race from Churchill Downs.

By the time Dino returned to say, "We have three long shots, numbers three, four, and eight, in the next pre-Derby race," Miami was swaying to the music.

The crowds at Agua Caliente were drunk, energetic, and loud as the race away showed the pre-Derby tight stretch run and desperate photo finish between horse number five and horse number eight. Moments later, the photo showed that Dino and Miami lost by a nose. Dino did not overreact to the loss. Losing by inches was an occupational hazard. He kept his emotions at an even keel.

Miami was sweating as time for the Derby drew close. He paced large circles around Dino, and Dino had to keep standing next to a floor-to-ceiling column where he had parked his oversized suitcase.

There was not a seat to be had anywhere.

And then, a surprise.

Big Bernie appeared in the race book in a bright yellow silk shirt and black Ray-Ban sunglasses. Dino asked him, "Who are you supposed to be? Madonna?" He also tried giving Big Bernie a hug, but Dino's arms were not long enough to complete the act.

Another man hug between Big Bernie and Miami happened and then Big Bernie told Dino, "Man, tell me she's going to win...I am so scared...it's like my whole life can change on this one race. I may have a heart attack just waiting."

Dino assured him, "I know she is the best horse, and if she has a clean trip, I believe she will win the race."

"Should I bet some money on another horse or two, just in case?" Bernie asked. "Who do you fear the most if she doesn't win?"

Dino said, "I think the only other speed horse is Forty Niner, and I pray he doesn't try to duel on the lead with her. I think her jockey, Pat Day, is too damn smart to try to sprint with her early and kill his own chances. But, the great thing is, he got a terrible post position outside, in the number 17 post. He has to lose ground into the first turn from way out there."

"Man, Forty Niner is like 6-1. Why don't I bet like four grand on him? If he beats her, I get back like 28 grand and lock in a profit even if she gets beat."

Miami raised an alarm. "Bernie, you can't do that," he said. "It will jinx her! Just stand pat and stay put! You've done everything you could do to put yourself in the best position to win. Big Bernie...man...you're like Winning Colors' coach! I remember hearing another coach, Jim Valvano, say, 'My only job is to put my players in position to succeed.' Big Bernie, man, you've done that! Dino has done that...we've done that! Just sit back and let it play out. You've done all you can do! It's up to the gods of horseracing now. Go have a mai tai!"

"I would...but my heart is racing too fast in my chest. Really, I'm not sure I can take this."

May 7, 1988, Churchill Downs Racetrack, Kentucky, 6:30 p.m.

In Louisville, Luis was proud to lead Winning Colors by her white halter onto the track in front of 150,000 fans. Gary Stevens was wearing the usual bright yellow silks with blue sleeves, and the bright yellow cap of the San Diego Chargers and the Klein Stable.

Luis had taken care of his gray filly nearly every day of her life and she was now calm in his presence.

The crowd sang, "My Old Kentucky Home," as the horses paraded in front of the fans. Singing the Kentucky state song has been a tradition since 1921, despite references in the lyrics to slavery. Just two years prior, in 1986, the Kentucky legislators replaced the song's original words "darky" and "darkies" with the word "people." Few singers were paying attention to such details.

In the moments before this race, the jockeys were more focused than they'd ever been in their lives, knowing the danger of piloting 17 animals, all 1,000-pounds-plus, all running simultaneously at 40 miles an hour. Stevens, now perched on top of Winning Colors, felt the enormity of the moment for himself and for his trainer, but he stayed focused on the proper way to warm up this filly. He wanted her on edge, to break and be alert; he did not want her to be nervous. His vision was to get her in front and out of traffic trouble in the huge field, and then rate her enough to conserve energy for the long stretch run to come down the stretch.

Gene Klein stood with Joyce in Millionaires Row. Oozing confidence, Klein remained fearless, believing he could win a Derby if his heart condition didn't flare. A representative from Dubai's ruling family, The Maktoum's, had offered $7,000,000 for the filly the previous week and he had responded with laughter telling Lukas, "The hell with them."

D. Wayne Lukas looked reserved and cool in his Armani suit, but he felt butterflies in his stomach. A Kentucky Derby win was the only professional goal he had yet to achieve. As he'd walked to the paddock, a fan called to Lukas: "You're zero for 13! Zero for 13!" Another race failure would be personally tough to endure, as would the professional criticism.

After saddling his filly, Lukas was too nervous to watch the two-minute race in a crowded area, which was in a private box with his wife, family, and the Kleins. He ducked into an alcove no bigger than a janitor's closet located near the racing secretary's office. It had a small, low-quality television screen.

A determined reporter who had been tracking him all day crammed himself in next to Lukas and asked, "How are you going to watch the race on that little screen?"

"She's gray. And she'll be in front the whole way," Lukas replied.

Stevens looked up into the stands. He saw women and girls holding up dozens of signs encouraging Winning Colors—and him!—to "Beat the Boys!" He heard their voices: "Go, Gary! You can do it!" Stevens felt a calm come over him as he led her in the post parade from the paddock onto the track in front of the fans. He looked down on his left sleeve, noticing a ladybug had landed on his yellow and blue silks. Strange… he thought. He then jogged Winning Colors vigorously to keep her focused and ready to break alert and take the lead.

The late afternoon sun was soft as the 17 Derby horses took time to enter the two gates set at the far-left end of the grandstand. Winning Colors loaded calmly into the number eight gate, as Stevens noticed that despite their warm-up run, the ladybug remained attached to his jersey.

Forty Niner was also in yellow silks in the number 17 post position, the second gate farthest out from the rail. Pat Day thought about how Forty Niner must not lose too much ground from this terrible post position closer to the fans than to the inside of the damn racetrack. Only one horse in Derby history had ever won from the outside auxiliary gate.

The final outside gates were loaded, the noise from 150,000 fans elevated to a growing low roar, and the flag was up. The gates popped open at the bell. The start resembled a cavalry charge with 68 hooves pawing at the Churchill Downs dirt, moving to establish positions for the long run into the first turn.

Winning Colors dug in her hindquarters and hurled herself onto the track, clawing and pulling the ground with her front legs, working to get to the front of the thundering wave of charging colts. Stevens hunched over her shoulders, urging her with his arms to accelerate. She was charging on the lead, sprinting away from the colts. She opened up a three-and-a-half-length lead past the grandstands the first time. Gary Stevens smiled as she took a commanding lead.

They were going to let her sneak away to a lonely lead!

Forty Niner broke fast as well and Pat Day steered him toward the filly, guiding his colt closer toward the inside part of the track, but still losing ground. He was forced to move from the number 17 lane to the number two lane. Forty Niner was now running in second position, just outside the huge gray filly, and she was skimming the rail.

Winning Colors was running away from them on the lead.

Pat Day had done the impossible already in getting Forty Niner to break perfectly and gently, without forcing his mount, and positioning just outside Winning Colors. Both horses saved some ground into the first left-hand turn.

Big Bernie, Miami, and Dino were staring at the television monitor surrounded by the surreal party crowd in Tijuana as Miami pumped his fist and yelled, "She's in front!" What would be the first quarter-mile time fraction? The three men wanted to see a time of 24 and change. When they saw it was 23 seconds flat, they were furious and worried.

Dino yelled at the screen, "What the hell is Stevens doing? Dammit, she can't run that fast early! It's suicide!"

Like Dino, Big Bernie and Miami knew this was terrible. This was one of their two worst fears. The first was she would break poorly and get shuffled back into traffic. She broke great, so they could check that off the nightmare list. Their second fear was the pace would be too fast early and she would just labor in the stretch like she had in her lone loss against Goodbye Halo. Winning Colors had now just set an insane opening quarter-mile fraction, so fast that the field was stretched out behind her 35 lengths from first to last, behind her torrid pace!

Day could tell the gray filly was going ridiculously fast and grabbed hold of Forty Niner, letting Winning Colors blast away to the lead on her own. He dropped Forty Niner back into the first turn.

The betting favorite was Private Terms, as the last flash on the betting tote board showed that Winning Colors was now just under 3.5-1 and Private Terms at 3-1. Private Terms had moved up into contention, but he was carried five horses wide into the first turn.

The Derby fans were rooting and cheering; especially the women. Fans had set a Derby record, betting $41 million on the race.

Again, Pat Day was aware Winning Colors was running too fast to survive the stretch, and he did an amazing thing, unseen in racing. He pulled Forty Niner back even more and allowed another horse to charge up inside of him and take over second place. Day had raced too many times in the Kentucky Derby to try to win now, so he had decided to save Forty Niner for when the real running began in the last quarter-mile.

Winning Colors was barreling down the backstretch now, distancing herself from the nearest males behind her by four open lengths! Forty Niner was losing ground to the other charging horses, as long shot Proper Reality also passed him on the inside. Day's mount dropped back to fourth.

Dave Johnson called over the public address system, "Winning Colors is in front and no one has challenged her yet! She has led from the start."

Miami and Dino noticed Forty Niner dropping back. Miami yelled, "Forty Niner is done! He spit the bit."

The time flashed up on the screen for the half-mile: 46-and-four-fifths seconds. Extremely fast, but not insane…better.

"Stevens is rating her," Dino yelled. There was still three-quarters-of-a-mile to run and she had to reserve her energy. Proper Reality was chasing her on the rail, moving strong. Stevens continued to sit still on Winning Colors. She was cruising fast and smooth. He sensed she was happy and was running within herself.

Stevens remembered the plan he and Lukas had made; a crazy, gutsy, unique plan—to try to steal the Kentucky Derby by winning it on the turn. Winning Colors had shown them she could run faster than the other champion 3-year-olds, and she was especially faster than them while running on the turns! This tall, leggy, athletic animal could accelerate in the turns when the other horses were spinning out and wasting energy.

In a moment that horserace fans still talk about, Winning Colors re-accelerated in the stretch turn, as if she has just broken away from the gate anew. She opened by six lengths on the 16 colts. Every woman and girl in the crowd screamed for the filly that was embarrassing the Derby colts as they entered the long, deep, tiring stretch for home.

Stevens urged Winning Colors with his arms and chirped to her in her left ear, "Let's go, girl! Now, girl! Now, girl. Go!" This was a bold move and could backfire if she couldn't build enough of a lead.

"She's led from the start…every pole a winning one!" the track announcer said.

The undefeated favorite, Private Terms, now gathered himself. His jockey, Chris Antley, set him down for a charge into the stretch.

Day, on Forty Niner, had gambled. He gambled that no filly could go this fast and last, and now he asked for all Forty Niner had! His colt was seasoned and a veteran of battles against the best colts in the world. He counted on the fact that Forty Niner would respond with courage and talent.

Winning Colors was running near the rail, and running for her life. Stevens was not reserving her at all. He was stealing the race then and there as he continued to urge her forward with his hands and arms. He spoke to her in rhythm with each stride. She reached forward with her front hooves pulling forward in huge, strong strides. When she was six lengths in front, Stevens felt her become exhausted.

This moment was subtle, but even Miami, Dino, and Big Bernie, 2,000 miles away, watching on a little television monitor at an iffy, chaotic foreign racetrack, could see it. They saw a slight shortening in her stride, as she drifted toward the inner rail, skimming against the paint, allowing the closers to run the firm, outside part of the racetrack.

Stevens didn't want her there! He wanted her out on the firm part of the track, where the closers would have to go wide and lose some ground to pursue her late. Stevens reached for his whip, took it in his left hand, and showed it to her, but did not hit her. He sensed she was still giving all she had in her body and heart. He felt Proper Reality closing ground and saw Forty Niner now flying on the outside.

Day reached for his whip with his left hand fully extended toward the sky. Whack! He hit Forty Niner hard. Again, and again, and again he tattooed Forty Niner, pausing just to show him the whip again. Under the whip's pressure, Forty Niner passed Proper Reality and accelerated, pouring himself into the track now, making up ground with every massive stride.

Stevens went to work with his whip on Winning Colors too, but with just short bursts to her rear left hip, wanting to stop her from diving down into the rail. He could tell she was all out but wanted her to keep focused to the wire. They were 100 yards from the finish line.

The announcer screamed, "Here comes Forty Niner, 2-year-old champ from last year, putting in a bid from outside. Down the stretch they come!"

Miami, Dino, and Big Bernie had seen thousands of races in their gambling careers. They could judge that Forty Niner's strides were making up too much ground on their dream filly. Would he catch her before she could get to the finish line wire?

With 300 feet remaining, she was still in front by three lengths, staggering toward the rail.

With 200 feet left, she was in front by one length, and Forty Niner was eating up the distance.

Winning Colors was gallant, out of energy, spent, and now she was lugging into the rail. She was going to be beaten…she felt and heard Forty Niner charging up to her on her right hind flank.

Pat Day had made one tiny mistake in an otherwise masterful performance from post number 17. He could have kept Forty Niner out toward the middle of the track where Winning Colors would not have heard or seen his climatic charge. He chose to come in and drift right on top of the filly. Perhaps Forty Niner was just too tired to run straight.

Just as the wire loomed before them, Winning Colors dug in again, and again, then, with her best effort, she pulled the ground toward her and lengthened her long, powerful, gorgeous body forward, and she stretched out to win by the length of her gray head.

CHAPTER 10

Drug Dogs

Some of the NBC TV cameras at the Kentucky Derby followed Winning Colors as she galloped out after her win. The other camera operators were searching for D. Wayne Lukas and his group's celebration. They couldn't find the winning trainer, but one of the operators found Eugene Klein celebrating with his hands above his head, giving the NFL referee's touchdown signal.

In reference to Klein, announcer Jim McKay said, "Football was never like this!"

Klein knew, after experiencing two heart attacks, this was likely his last chance for a Derby win and it was the greatest sporting moment he could imagine. Klein accepted the trophy saying, "I would really like to salute all the women in America...this one is for all you gals."

A reporter asked him," Mr. Klein how many races have you won? And how much money?"

"I don't really know, but we have won over 300 races and over $25,000,000 in purses."

"Have you made a profit in racing now?"

"I think so...if you discount what my wife has bet!"

Lukas was still in the small out-of-the-way alcove. He'd achieved the most difficult training accomplishment in the world of horse racing—going from training cheap quarter horses in South Dakota in 1967, to the Winner's Circle in the 1988 Kentucky Derby. At age 57, there was nothing in the world of American horse training that he had left to do. He wanted to run to his wife Shari, and to his family, and to the Kleins, but mostly he wanted to run to his son Jeff, to celebrate what they had accomplished together. In that emotional moment, he worked to absorb that he had just won the one race that had eluded him on his quest to be the greatest trainer in American history. He let it sink in.

He then stood tall and walked with elegance to the Winner's Circle. Every person he saw on the way congratulated him, and the fans cheered him as he arrived into their view.

He saw his son Jeff, and Luis. Both were walking Winning Colors to the Winner's Circle. They were surrounded by hundreds of people, all giving congratulations.

As a camera operator found him, Lukas hugged his son and raised Jeff's fist into the air. Lukas addressed the national television audience: "I want to thank my son. He did it…and he worked so hard. This is for all our guys…we are on top of the world…and we are looking down!"

As Gary Stevens dismounted, he saw his friend, jockey Jacinto Vasquez, who yelled to him, "I guess you do know how to win a Derby!"

Stevens came to the infield, to the NBC stage. He looked like a million dollars as he took off his helmet. Every hair was in place as he explained, "I asked her at the quarter pole for her life…and she gave it to me! We tried to steal it…and that's what we did! The last 25 seconds of the race were the longest 25 seconds of my life."

He then accepted the keys to a new car for an added victory bonus.

Luis had found a good vantage point to watch the race on the ground near the horse tunnel. When his Mamacita crossed the wire, he exploded in joy, jumping up and down again, and again. Then he rushed down to the track to await her triumphant return to the Winner's Circle. He knew that she did not like to be in crowds. He pushed the fans away from her and gave her space with his arms before he draped a heavy blanket of fresh red roses over her neck. Only then did he kneel and make the sign of the cross, then wept tears of joy.

In his mind's eye, he saw her as a baby 2-year-old frolicking on her back in her stall, the times he gave her treats, the times he'd given her fresh straw every night before he left her stall, and the times he traveled with her across the country to keep her safe. His tears spilled for each day that she'd come back to him uninjured from competition and training.

He cried for all the good ways that Winning Colors, Mamacita, had changed his life.

Mr. Lukas would likely have other chances to be in the Winner's Circle of the Kentucky Derby. But for Luis, born into poverty in Mexico, Winning Colors had been his one chance to win the ultimate race. His family and friends had watched him on national television as he walked the filly into the Winner's Circle.

Tucked away in his wallet was the Caesars Palace Futures 100-1 bet ticket. It was now worth $200,000. I'm going to need a bigger box in our closet, he thought.

Miami, Dino, and Big Bernie exploded in celebration as Winning Colors crossed the finish line in front. They hugged each other and then hugged the Mexican cowboys next to them. Miami found Camila and hugged her. He asked her to bring margaritas for everybody.

Dino's big white suitcase was the center of their attention. They were ready to stuff it with as many hundred-dollar bills as it would allow. Dino couldn't stand still. He was hopping around like a jumping bean. "She did it!" he yelled. "She is the best 3-year-old in the country! I told you six months ago!"

Miami confirmed it. "You did! You are a track god! Who do you like in the next race?"

The Tijuana party wound itself down. Tequila had been flowing into the gamblers and revelers for many hours. Bets and cocktails had separated most of the gamblers from the money in their pockets. Dino and Miami still sat, enjoying their margaritas. Big Bernie stood next to them.

"Big Bernie, did you bet your $20,000 in one betting ticket, or multiple smaller tickets?" Dino asked.

"I made it into four $5,000 smaller bets each. I brought only one of them with me today to cash today with my buddies. Holy shit. I didn't really want to think about it. Didn't want to jinx it. I just realized that ticket is now worth…$250,000." Big Bernie plopped his huge frame down on a chair.

Miami realized the win was just setting in on Big Bernie's consciousness. He also knew that winning $1 million cannot be processed instantly by anyone. Big tears were coming out of the corners of Big Bernie's eyes. Miami noticed and said, "We did it, Bernie."

"Guys, I want you to come with me tonight to see the motel I'm buying. It's so awesome, right on the water, and my office…it's upstairs on the corner…white trim with a drop-dead view of the Pacific Ocean. You can see the whales from there like every day. We will stay there tonight. You gotta join me, boys!"

Dino was quick to answer. "We would like to, but I don't feel safe here holding winning tickets on Winning Colors worth $250,000. I want it to calm down in here just a little, get our money, and get back to LA. We'll come back and stay with you someday soon. I promise."

"Man, you will never have to pay. You come down and you can have the biggest rooms with views, on me, for life!"

"Thanks, that's great, thanks. But what's the plan now? When do we cash our tickets and get the fuck out of here?" Dino was ready to leave.

"I don't know," said Miami. He looked around. "I'm living a moment right here…give me a minute."

The race book was thinning out now, and the cocktail waitresses were picking up used glasses from the tables.

"You guys stay here. I'm going to go out and move my car and park it right out front. Then I say Dino goes up and cashes one ticket. When they start paying him, then Bernie and I'll go up to two other windows and cash our tickets. Big Bernie, where are you going to put $250,000? Into your pockets? And where did you park your car?"

"I took a cab from the border," he said. "I was planning on watching the Derby alone in my apartment. I really didn't plan it out. But then, I thought it would be lonely, you know, winning all this money by myself. So, I woke up and headed across the border to watch and celebrate with…well, I was hoping to see you guys. I'll drive back over the border with you. I don't really want to get into a cab now with $250,000 on me…alone."

Miami couldn't believe it. "I only have a two-seater Z!" he said. "You can't come with us! We have the suitcase that barely fits, and it'll be full of money too! Let me go move my car while I figure this out."

In the few minutes it took to move his car, Miami came up with a plan. He was eager to share it as soon as he got back to his friends. "Big Bernie, don't cash your ticket. Just take a cab back to the border. You'll be safe as long as they don't see you cash the ticket."

"OK. I trust you," said Big Bernie. "Whatever you say."

Miami now looked at Dino. "Go cash a $50,000 ticket. When they start paying you, I'll go to the window down the line, and cash out for $100,000. Then you go to another window and cash the remaining $100,000. Put it in the suitcase and we'll book it for the US border like bats out of hell."

Dino was thinking about where to get the cash into the suitcase without making a scene.

Miami continued with his plan. "Big Bernie, I think you should leave us now. Once we have that kind of money on us, we are toxic to you. As soon as we leave the building, catch the first cab and get the hell back to the US. I'll call you when we get back there tonight. Then I'll help you with the attorney that will get you your check for your $1 million."

Next, Miami called Camila over and paid his bill. She seemed afraid to be too near him now, but then whispered, "Be careful, Miami. They know you guys. Do not trust them."

The hairs on the back of Miami's neck went up when he heard this. Camila apparently knew more about what was going on than he thought, and her English was better than she let on.

He told Dino, "Go get the cash, Dino. Do it now!"

Dino went to a cashier's window and told the teller, "I have a big Derby futures ticket to cash. I want $100 bills, please."

The teller looked at the ticket, opened his mouth in a startled expression, and told him, "Un momento, por favor," and left to go into the back room. Miami and Big Bernie were watching from the other side of the room.

Several minutes passed.

The older man with the gold tooth who had been there in January returned. He was wearing a cheap dark brown suit and burnt orange tie.

"Señor, you need to come back later," said the man with the gold tooth.

"Later? When…like in an hour?"

"No…not today. Possible mañana."

Dino's voice rose much louder, "What the fuck are you talking about? Manana my ass. Look…the ticket says, 'Winning Colors to win the 1988 Kentucky Derby.' She just won the race and I want my fucking money!" Dino waved Miami to come over, while Big Bernie stayed seated.

Miami came over and Dino said loudly, "They want us to come back another day. I'm telling him she won today. Today was the Derby, and we want to be paid. Today. Now!"

Miami looked at the manager and asked him, "Who is in charge? I want to see him now."

"Si, señor, un momento…."

He was gone for five minutes, then ten. Dino looked at Miami and said, "I don't like this. The place is getting too quiet now. How can they not pay us?"

Finally, the older man returned with the handsome younger man who looked like a Mexican version of Elvis. Four security guards came into view, with rifles shouldered on their backs. The younger man spoke, "There is no problem, señors. But you must come back another day to collect. We are not prepared today for such a thing."

"You were damn well prepared to take our money. You should be damn well prepared to pay the winners!" Dino shouted as he put his face within six inches of the lead guard's face. The other security guards moved closer to the gamblers.

"Leave him alone! When should we come back?" Miami asked.

"Posiblemente mañana. Call us first," said Mexican Elvis.

Miami looked at Dino and said, "Let's go. We are bringing Big Bernie with us. We can't leave him here."

"How can we fit him in your car?"

"I don't know, put him on your lap, I don't care. We can't leave him here with these liars! I am so fucking pissed! You can't take our gambling money and not pay us. Man, that's against the gamblers' code. They know that. Fuck them."

They walked over to Big Bernie and said, "They won't pay us today. We have to leave…now…fast…let's go. Let's go. I don't trust them. You have to come with us…don't take a cab, Bernie. It's not safe! Let's go! Now!"

Big Bernie looked at Miami and held up both his palms to the sky. "What do we do now, Miami?"

Miami pointed in the direction they had to run.

They jogged off the betting floor, down the stairs of the grand old racetrack. Dino was dragging the empty suitcase, and Big Bernie was struggling to keep up. They heard the loud heavy footsteps of several security guards now rushing to catch up to them on the stairs. On the lower floor, more guards were watching them while talking on their radios. Miami looked back and saw that two of the four guards seen at the cashiers' windows were now following them.

They slowed the pace and Miami took his chance to say to Dino in a low voice, "We have $250,000 worth of winning tickets on us, plus Bernie's $250,000 ticket. We can't let these guards anywhere near us... they'll steal the tickets. Run!"

Big Bernie was now moving faster as they sprinted down the marble lined floors, out the main entrance doors, to the Z. Miami jumped in and fired up the turbo engine. Big Bernie stopped, saw two small seats, and looked at Dino.

Dino yelled, "This isn't going to work. Miami! Put the top down."

Miami got out to take the convertible hardtop roof off and store it in the back. He tossed the white suitcase out and left it in the parking lot.

Big Bernie squeezed his huge frame into the small car, tried to put on the seat belt, but it wouldn't fit over him. Dino leaped into his lap; his head was sticking one foot over the roof line of the convertible. "Let's roll!" Dino yelled.

Miami got in, put on his seat belt and his fingerless leather racing gloves, checked his rear-view mirror, saw the guards coming toward the car, and hit the throttle hard. The turbo boost kicked in at 20 mph, and Miami hit 60 before he exited the parking lot, while driving over the curb. He raced up the avenue toward the US border. Over the wind noise in the convertible, Miami yelled, "Is anyone following us? Keep looking. I need to know if you see anyone following us between here and the border. These fuckers are not catching me!"

Miami was driving like it was the last lap at a Formula 1 race, weaving through and around slow-moving cars and the noisy, lumbering trucks. When he got to a red light, he merely slowed, then hit the gas, and ran the light. He hit the main avenue, Paseo de los Héroes, at 93 mph as he looked over and saw Dino's face getting pummeled by the air flow. Miami saw that Big Bernie's eyes were bulging, but…he was smiling.

"Man…I love you guys!" Big Bernie yelled. "I'll never forget this day…ever…!"

Big Bernie was dropped off at his car where it was parked just across the border. The drive back to Los Angeles for Miami and Dino was done mostly in silence. Bernie agreed to call later and meet Miami and Dino the next morning at nine a.m. for a Sunday breakfast at the café.

Amalia and Ava joined the three of them at the breakfast. They all looked ragged from the adventure and a lousy night's sleep, but the women looked great, ready for a day together at the beach.

It was time to brainstorm. They needed a plan to collect the money. It was agreed that $1,000,000 in cash was too much cash to risk. Big Bernie wanted to stay with his plan and get a check cut to his Mexican attorney's banking account. Big Bernie was still cash-flush from his Pick 6 score but did admit to Miami and Dino he had lost about $30,000 since then in the Santa Anita Pick 6 betting pools.

All three men were angry that the track's owner had broken the code.

"You always pay your gambling debts first," Miami told them. "I think this proves they are going out of business. If they didn't pay us, then they didn't pay maybe hundreds of other smaller bettors on Winning Colors. When this news gets out, that track will be toast. Nobody will ever go there and bet again."

"Nobody goes there now. Simulcasting is killing them from Del Mar," said Big Bernie. "They probably don't even care."

"I'm going back to get my money. Our money," said Dino. "They can't do this to honest, hard-working gamblers. I'll sue them."

"Can you sue the cartel?" Miami asked. "We can't go back there alone…not like yesterday. I don't think taking an armored car works. If they are going to rob us…then they are going to rob us. I see only four scenarios: One: They pay us, and we go on our way. Two: They file bankruptcy in Mexico. Big Bernie, ask your Tijuana attorney about this. Three: They set us up with some local banditos…you know…not professional guys…they pay us…then just have some locals knock us off and split the money with them. Four: We are dealing with real cartel guys here…in which case we are dead. Period."

Amalia and Ava looked at the men. They were horrified. Ava said, "Maybe you can hire some off-duty Los Angeles cops or something to go with you."

"I have a guy who knows professional fighters," said Dino. "I've never seen them, but my buddies go to their matches all the time. These guys like…they mix regular boxers with kickboxers and karate and shit."

"I heard those guys are badass. Remember when Muhammed Ali fought against some wrestler guy, and they fought to a draw…but Ali got really messed up?" said Big Bernie.

"OK, Dino. Set them up." Miami was serious. "Get three of them. My plan is for Dino and me to go in my car, and we hire these professional fighters to drive Dino's Impala to help collect the money."

"No way you guys are going without me!" Big Bernie said as he jumped, nearly spilling his coffee over Amalia and Ava. "You guys stayed with me, and I'm going with you guys for sure. End of story."

Miami looked at Dino and said, "Big Bernie you shouldn't risk your life on this. Man, you're going to be rich, and should be done with all of this…forever."

"No. No way. It's the three of us, and we are seeing this thing through together, man. All the way. I'm coming with you."

"OK, OK. You're in…you crazy son of a bitch! I'm giving you a new nickname when this is over…Kick Ass Bernie."

"Don't take the Impala, guys. It's not working well," added Dino.

Miami had another idea. "I know a guy who works with me. He owes me. He has a four-door Camry. He'll loan it to us, and I'll drive my Z."

"Guys…I don't like any of this," Amalia said. "Can't you just forget the whole thing? Dino, you told me you liked the races because the horses were so pretty…and now you're gambling with cartel guys? I'm just a librarian, but I'm Mexican. You don't understand what it's like in Mexico. They run the place. They own the police and the politicians. Guys, please don't go…it's not worth the risk."

Amalia was now in tears.

Later that day, Dino called Agua Caliente racetrack to find out the days and times when the cashiers' windows were open. Dino didn't want to alert them as to when they were coming back, but they planned to go Thursday morning at 9:00 a.m. It had dawned on Miami that maybe three tough fighters whom he'd never met were also a threat to their $250,000 windfall, but he just couldn't go there now, and put the thought aside.

May 12, 1988, Westwood, California, and Tijuana, Mexico

Thursday arrived clear and hot. Big Bernie, Dino, and Miami waited at the café rear parking lot as planned. Miami arranged to borrow the Toyota from a fellow real estate broker he knew, who was more interested in drinking and taking drugs than caring about loaning his car to people who'd drive it into Mexico. They were waiting for the arrival of their bodyguards, the "fighters," or, "The Muscle," as they called them.

Dino and Big Bernie were in a disagreement as to who had to make the day's 10-hour drive with the professional fighters to and from Mexico.

Miami told Big Bernie that having Dino drive would add three hours to the trip because he drove so damn slowly. Big Bernie agreed to pilot the mercenaries back and forth across the border. Miami was paying the three fighters $250 each for the trip.

"I hope these big guys fit in the Camry."

To pass the time, Miami showed off his latest purchase—a small Motorola cell phone. It weighed less than four pounds and did not have to be connected to a battery pack for the first 45 minutes of calling. He gave Big Bernie the phone number but cautioned him it was three dollars per minute of talk time; "...so don't call for fun."

The professional fighters showed up 20 minutes late. They arrived in a beat-up, lime colored, four-door Isuzu sedan, with the radio antenna hanging off the side of the right bumper. Three young Asian men got out and walked over to the men. The tallest of them was five-foot-five, and he towered over the other two. Miami looked at Dino and the laughter began. Big Bernie joined in laughing so hard he had to lean on Miami's car to hold himself up.

"Man!" said Miami, "we have nothing to worry about from those cartel guys now, huh Dino?"

"The track will probably pay us extra, just so we don't hurt them," said Big Bernie, as they continued to laugh.

The fighters saw the gamblers laughing at them. They didn't like it. The tallest came forward and put his face six inches from Miami's face. "You think we can't fight, surfer dude? I kick your ass right now! Right here."

"Take it easy…take it easy, man. We were just expecting some… you know…big guys to scare people with. I'm sure you could kick my ass. I'm sorry…you just don't look like bouncers."

"You pay us to go, or you pay us not to go. We don't care," said the tallest fighter.

"Give me a minute to talk to my guys," said Miami as he huddled up with Dino and Big Bernie away from the fighters. "Guys, what do we do? These three aren't going to scare anyone from messing with us."

Dino said, "They are really dangerous guys, Miami. One of them…I don't know which…I think the short one…is a Brazilian Tae Kwon Do champion, and undefeated."

"Which one is the short one? What weight class? Ninety pounds and under?" asked Big Bernie as he and Miami tried to stop laughing.

Dino wasn't laughing. "Miami…stop it…they are going to beat the shit out of us. We gotta pay them either way…it can't hurt to take 'em with us."

So, they put the three fighters in the gold Toyota with Big Bernie and headed south to Mexico to collect their cash.

Several hours later, they were all in the car insurance office in San Diego to buy two policies—one for each car. This time, when Miami insured a six-year-old Toyota Camry for $200,000 for twenty-four hours of coverage, he was again met with skepticism.

Miami had heard the fighters' Asian real names but could not remember or pronounce them. He'd renamed them Jimmy, Choo, and Peanut. Over a lunch of cheeseburgers, they planned their ticket-cashing plan, and called it "Operation Gringo."

Operation Gringo went into effect the second they crossed the border into Mexico. Miami led the elite team into the Agua Caliente parking lot. It was all but empty on Thursday at 2:00 p.m. as they backed the two cars into front-exit-facing positions. Dino went to the Camry and brought out eight large green backpacks he'd purchased. He intended to ask for $20 bill denominations this time.

They left the cars and headed for a cashier window cage on the betting floor, and it was there that Dino asked where he could cash a "futures bet." The cashier pointed down the hall to an office. They followed the directions to find what resembled a bank, with thick metal bars on the front two windows, and a half-dozen employees in the back office area.

Big Bernie and Choo stayed outside in the main race book as lookouts. Dino brought out a $2,000 ticket now worth $100,000 and handed it to the clerk. "Please pay in US $20 bills...thank you."

The clerk held one finger up and left the cage. He came back in under one minute with an older man who said, "You need to come back into the office. *El jefe* wants to talk to you. Just you two."

Dino looked at Miami. "I don't like it."

"What else can we do?"

Dino and Miami followed the older man and two guards down a long hallway, deep into the old racetrack, then down two flights of stairs, and into a large dark room, with one light bulb dangling from the ceiling and an old, beat-up fan on a desk. The guards stayed out in the hallway. A large Mexican man was sitting at the table, smoking a fat cigar, and filling the small enclosure with heavy smoke. There were no chairs for the two gamblers to sit.

"Buenos dias, señors. I see you are back with us again."

"We are good customers," said Miami. "We are thinking of moving to Tijuana."

"Don't get smart with me. Do you know who you are dealing with?"

"We know who the fuck you are," said Dino. "And we know about El Gato's murder, and about who is the main suspect. We contacted the *LA Times* and told them we are coming today...and when and why... they even have copies of our betting tickets...if we disappear you are going to have a real international problem! The front page of the *LA* fucking *Times*...and the *San Diego Tribune*. Your boss is going to be on the fucking cover...so do whatever you want...but it will be the god damn end of this track and its owner."

The man looked at Miami. "Tell your little friend here to calm down...and don't talk shit to me. How much money did you bet on her?"

"Not much...like $5,000. Nothing for a huge place like yours."

"I think you bet much more. Do not lie to us. We want to be fair."

Dino walked right up to his face. "Then pay us! You took our money to win the Derby. We won. Stop this shit."

The man smiled at Miami, and said, "Tell your small friend to calm down. We are businessmen. We think that you bet over $25,000...so you won like $1,250,000. That's a lot of money in Tijuana. We want you to be safe...we can give you the money in pesos."

"No fucking way!" Dino shouted. "We bet US dollars and you're re going to pay us in US dollars."

Miami said, "Hell...we will probably lose most of it back this year. We only want to cash a $250,000 ticket today."

The man's eyebrows went up. He nodded his head. He pursed his lips. "Only $250,000? You are some rich gringos if $250,000 is small to you."

"I told you, we are good customers."

The man left for over 20 minutes. Dino began to pace circles in the small office. Miami sat down in the man's chair, reached for a fresh, big cigar laying on the table, and lit it, blowing the rich smoke into the dark room.

"Don't smoke those things, they are bad for you."

Miami began to laugh. "We are in a member of the Tijuana Cartel's dungeon, trying to collect a quarter million from these guys...and you are worried about my smoking habits?... Man... where did you think of that *LA Times* story? Brilliant."

"It just came to me."

Finally, the man reappeared. "Señors, we never want to see you here again. Ever."

"Agreed," said Miami.

The older man led them back up the steps to the bank-like area, taking them to a teller's countertop. Miami whispered to Dino, "I think he was worried we were going to collect on Bernie's $1 million too."

At the teller's window the older man used a key to open a drawer below their line of sight. The man pulled up dozens of stacks of $20 bills, bound by paper wrappers printed with the words "Agua Caliente." The clerk next to the man asked in passable English, "Do you want to count each stack, señors?"

Dino looked at Miami and Miami nodded his head side-to-side.

"Señor, each stack has 100 bills. There are 100 $20 bills per stack, or 2,000 US dollars."

The clerk then counted 50 stacks of $20 bundles. Dino fanned through each one briefly to confirm they were all filled with $20 bank notes. He filled one backpack with $40,000 in cash, and then another. He put $20,000 in a third backpack and let Miami get to the front of the window.

Miami handed the clerk another $2,000 face value ticket. Under the watchful eye of the older man, the clerk counted out another 50 stacks of $20 bill bundles. Miami fanned them, then handed them to Dino who had now filled five backpacks, totaling $200,000.

Miami handed him the third and final $1,000 face value ticket on Winning Colors.

"Señors...we do not have more $20 bills. We will pay you in hundreds," said the older man, "un momento, por favor."

Then he went out of their view. They waited for five minutes. Miami smelled the scent of fear and sweat coming from his own body. He whispered to Dino, "I want to get the money and get the hell out of here."

The man came back carrying a brown burlap bag with an Agua Caliente logo on the side. He set it down with a heavy thud in front of the young clerk. The clerk deftly counted out five stacks of $100 bills, each with 100 bills per stack, and handed them to Miami. He placed them in a sixth backpack.

With this transaction over, Miami gave a $100 bill to each of the men. "*Muchas gracias*, gentlemen." Then Miami saw a guard with a rifle over his shoulder standing outside the counting room and handed him a $100 bill. Miami motioned the guard to follow as he and Dino exited.

Before they left the counting room, Miami stopped with Dino. They had agreed that Dino would pull a $100 bill out of each stack of bills from a $40,000 backpack, and he handed that backpack to Big Bernie as they re-entered the main race book.

When they got there, Miami looked at Big Bernie and Dino, smiled, and said, "Come on guys…we have time for just one grande margarita."

Big Bernie smiled and nodded a "yes." Dino scowled and threw three of the backpacks onto his shoulder and headed straight out the giant main archway toward the cars, with his two partners, plus Jimmy, Choo, and Peanut now fanned behind him, and the armed Mexican guard walking alongside Miami.

They loaded into the cars. Big Bernie reached into the backpack Dino had given to him and gave each of the three fighters a $9,900 stack of money to hold and take across the border. Miami let Big Bernie drive the Camry out first from the Agua Caliente parking lot to head for the US border. He and Dino followed in the Z right behind.

Everyone on Operation Gringo had been assigned where to look—front, to the roadway sides, and rear—for fear of an ambush on the way from the racetrack to the US border. They initially headed into light traffic but as they approached the international line, traffic was a near standstill. Miami's eyes were darting to every car behind him, watching for a door to open, and men to come out of it. They were now stopped dead, as the traffic was not even inching toward the border. He noticed a van behind him that had also made the same last few turns and lane changes as the Z.

"Shit. How can the traffic be like this on a Thursday afternoon?" Miami asked. Without waiting for an answer, he asked Dino another, more important question. "Are you sure you're OK with not declaring the cash with customs?"

"I've waited my entire life for this score, and I'm not declaring the money. We look pretty clean…like tourists. I'm sure they'll wave us through. I'm way more worried about Big Bernie, Jimmy, Choo, and Peanut. They look sketchy even to me."

"What do you want to do if they don't make it through?"

"We have to move on," said Miami. "They're behind us now and we can't turn around once we have $200,000 clean and through the border. But…I know. We can't leave Big Bernie. He is doing this for us…not for him."

The cars were now moving, crawling toward the border, and street vendors were coming up to them one after another. A man in his mid-twenties, with tattoos on his arms and neck, was at Dino's window, motioning him to roll it down.

"Don't even look at him," said Miami.

The guy was persistent and stayed with them as they moved forward. Dino rolled down the window three inches. "Get the fuck out of here," Dino yelled at him through the window crack.

The guy left.

A boy hopped onto the hood of the car and began to clean the front windshield. Miami reached through the window, gave him a $20 bill, and motioned him to go away. He smiled and ran off.

Miami steered the car toward the "US Citizens Only" lanes, where no passports or IDs were required, unless tourists were stopped for further questioning. Miami saw what looked like a US Customs guard standing in between the rows of cars, wearing aviator glasses and a bulletproof vest, peering into cars and talking into his radio. As they pulled next to him, Miami waved to him…and the agent waved him by.

"Big Bernie is two cars behind us, Miami."

The Z was in a line behind 20 cars at the customs booths. The "San Ysidro Port of Entry" sign could be seen overhead as the cars were now led into 17 lanes, with 17 sets of US Border Agents at each crossing point. Dozens of other agents were standing behind them with German Shepherds on leashes. Miami reached down and turned on a Mexican radio station at high volume.

"Stop that shit! Quit fucking around!" said Dino as he turned the radio off.

"Hey, I don't look Mexican…I'll be fine… You, I'm not so sure." Miami was smiling and laughing as they came up to the customs agents. The two customs agents barely looked at the Z and waved them on through.

Dino's eyes—Miami's too—were each looking into a side view mirror, focused on Big Bernie's Camry two cars behind. Miami rolled into the right emergency lane to wait for the Camry to be waved through.

The Camry inched forward, and two US Customs agents motioned Big Bernie to stop. The agents circled the car and then two more appeared and wheeled a device with mirrors on it under the Camry. Another agent brought a drug-sniffing dog around the car. The German Shepherd leaped and barked, pulling aggressively against his leash, showing his teeth, and trying to get into the car. The dog had found something, and he was desperate to get to it fast. The agent nearest Big Bernie told him to move the car to the right where a large dual-language sign read "Secondary Inspection/Inspection Secundaria." The inspection area was under a covered awning 30 yards away from the main border checkpoint. The Camry's occupants were now in the United States of America.

Razor sharp barbed wire fronted the car. Metal poles on each side separated each vehicle stall area. Three customs agents with hand-held rifles stared down at them. An agent walked up to Big Bernie and yelled, "Stay put in the car."

"Yes, sir."

A second agent came around the car. He was surveying the fighters and the car's interior with a long black flashlight. Its light was shining through the windows, despite the daylight. His other hand was firm on the pistol handle on his right hip.

"All of you," said the agent, "please step out of the car."

The German Shepherd was allowed to enter the car, on leash. It barked, just inches from the ashtray. The customs agent holding the leash opened the ashtray and found remnants of two marijuana joints left there by the car's owner.

The fighters and Bernie complied with the directions they were given. The four were escorted into a building with bars on the windows and razor wire around the perimeter. They were seated on a bench under the eyes of two agents with rifles drawn. The second agent with the nametag "Contreras," asked them, "Do you speak English?"

"No," said Jimmy.

"Nope," said Choo.

Peanut did not respond.

Bernie smiled and said, "I do."

"Come with me." Big Bernie was led down the hallway into a large room where he was asked to strip down to his underwear. He was patted down and searched. He then followed directions to put the contents of his pockets onto the counter. Moments later Big Bernie stood there in his boxer shorts, with $9,900 on the counter, and freezing in the air-conditioned holding cell. Contreras interviewed him for 20 minutes then left him alone. But...Contreras took the money.

Next Jimmy was given the same treatment, and again placed $9,900 in twenty-dollar bills on the counter. When asked questions by the border agent he replied in broken Cantonese dialect, "I work for Mr. Big." He refused to answer more questions. When they asked, he shook his head from side to side.

The same scenario played out for Choo. "I work for Mr. Big. Ask him...I not speak English."

Peanut, dressed only in his underwear, put his $9,900 on the counter and didn't respond to questions. After 10 minutes, agent Contreras gave up on talking with the diminutive fighters. He had no idea where he could find a Cantonese interpreter in a US/Mexico border customs office.

The fighters were then left locked in cold, small detention rooms, each alone.

Miami and Dino sat on the side of the 805 Freeway as hundreds of cars accelerated past them toward San Diego. "There goes $40,000," said Dino.

Miami clenched his hands, and then banged his fists together. "Man! What about Big Bernie? Man, we can't leave him. He is there because of us. We can't go back with $200,000 in cash on us. What do we do now?"

"We can't sit here, Miami. I'm sure we are raising suspicions by just sitting here."

"Yeah...you're right."

After several minutes Miami said, "OK, Dino...you take the car, the cell phone, and the money and go to Del Mar racetrack. There are lots of guards there, and cops. You and the money will be safe. I'll walk back and try to get them out. If they call you from customs, remember we won $10,000 each. That's it. Got it?"

"How will you get to Del Mar?"

"We'll figure it out. Give me $2,000 and go. Now. Fast. And don't gamble there, buddy."

Miami took the money from Dino, exited the car, and walked back toward the border crossing.

The border agents watched Miami closely as he approached, and then led him into the main office. "Ah, you must be Mr. Big. So glad you came back. Why do they have drugs in the car?" asked Agent Contreras.

"Who's Mr. Big? What are you talking about? Drugs? The fighters have drugs on them?"

Contreras's brow wrinkled, and he crossed his arms. He then pointed a finger directly at Miami's face. "Fighters? These guys are like Asian terrorists or something?"

"No. No. No. Well…yeah…they are professional fighters but not like terrorists…today they are just protecting me."

Agent Contreras interviewed Miami and heard the story of Winning Colors. All facts—except for the amount they had wagered, bringing the total bet amount down to $1,200.

Agent Contreras knocked his closed fist on the table several times and looked hard at Miami. "So, OK. OK…let me get this straight. Mr. Big…you are really named Miami, you each have thousands of dollars in cash on you…and have three paid professional fighters as full-time body guards to protect you…with drugs in their car…and you are crossing the US/Mexican border on a Thursday afternoon…and I'm supposed to believe it's all because you bet on a mare to win the Kentucky Derby? You are going to be here for a while. Like for years, Mr. Big."

"She's a filly, not a mare. She's only 3-years-old."

The three fighters and Big Bernie had been pulled from the car about 3:30 p.m., and it was now approaching 8:00 p.m. Miami could hear Agent Contreras talking on the phone from the neighboring office because the door was open. "Yep, we have some surfer guy dressed like Don Johnson here, and some Italian guy named Dino that got away and is holding out at Del Mar racetrack. Then we have three Chinese professional fighter bodyguards that claim not to speak English, and some huge guy name Big Bernie. They have $39,600 on them and the dogs found a bunch of old marijuana roach butts in the ashtray. Yeah. That's about it."

The supervisor—or some official on the other end—spoke for a while, because Contreras went silent.

Contreras then asked, "What about the money?"

Silence. Then, Contreras said, "OK. Got it, boss."

Agent Contreras went to the back of the complex, and came back in 20 minutes with Big Bernie, Jimmy, Choo, and Peanut. All were dressed. He handed a large envelope with $39,600 in it to Miami and said, "You are all free to go."

Big Bernie broke into a wide smile and put his fist into the air.

Peanut, suddenly remembering English, smiled and looked at Agent Contreras and said, "Thank you very much, Agent Contreras."

They all buckled up in the Camry with Miami driving, Big Bernie in the passenger seat, and all three fighters stuffed in the rear.

"We didn't tell them anything Miami, not even your name, boss," Jimmy said, as Choo and Peanut nodded their heads and smiled.

They headed for Del Mar racetrack. A bit later, Miami stopped to call Dino who answered on the small new cell phone.

"We lost all the money, man," he said. "Big Bernie's in prison and the fighters are being extradited. We need you to come back down immediately and pay our bail."

CHAPTER 11

Mariachi Madness

Dino's new black Lincoln Continental wound its way down Highway 10 from the US border toward Rosarito, Mexico. The town's coastline was pristine, with blue waves and white foam breaking onto its wide sandy beaches. Miami was driving, and Ava was in the front seat next to him, trying to read a Mexican map resting on top of her long white skirt. Amalia and Dino sat in the back seats.

"Where the hell is this motel, anyway?" said Miami.

It's now a hotel, not a motel. It has a restaurant and a bar," said Ava. "I think you turn right here. Yes…head toward the beach, it says." Ava was reading from the wedding invitation that she'd helped design:

Te Invitamos a Celebrar Nuestra Boda
We Invite You to Celebrate Our Wedding
Isabel Cuevas
and
Don Bernie
Saturday, the eighth of April 1989
Half past five in the afternoon
Winning Colors Hotel
Rosarito Beach, Mexico

They pulled onto a long driveway with bright white fencing that swept up to a two-story white stucco building with a large yellow and blue sign: The Winning Colors Hotel. Valet parking attendants in white pants and shirts took over parking the Lincoln as Bernie ran down steps from the bar to meet them. "Miami, Dino, Ava, Amalia! Welcome to your second home, my amigos!" He put his long arms nearly around them all at the same time and squeezed with the enthusiasm of an old friend.

"Big Bernie! We're so happy to see you again!" said Miami.

"It's not Big Bernie anymore. First…you can see I've lost 30 pounds. Isabel makes them cook healthy for me. I am now Don Bernie. I am a land baron…and a hotel owner, and a restaurant owner, and a bar owner. Show a little damn respect, Miami…I can have you arrested at any time here in my city, amigo."

"Si…Don Bernie…lo siento Mr. Don Bernie," shouted Miami as they all headed to the bar.

The bar sat atop a bluff looking down at the Pacific Ocean. A lovely young woman in a bright floral Mexican dress was singing a familiar song, but in Spanish, and with a twist: "The Boy from Ipanema." A young man playing a keyboard accompanied her. Don Bernie ordered grande margaritas for everyone—tart, strong, salt on the rims cutting into the tequila—perfect for the hot weather that day.

"When do we get to meet Isabel? I want to spend some time warning her about Miami's bad influence on you and Dino," said Ava.

"Not until tonight of course. You are going to love her, Ava. Dino, you will too. Miami…she is way too smart for you and probably won't like you."

The wedding was small, just 40 guests, and over half were from Isabel's family. Don Bernie had hired nearly as many staff as guests, with three young bartenders making margaritas, servers passing hors d'oeuvres, and a kitchen full of chefs. At the end of the pool and bar was a white pagoda with trellises covered in red, yellow, and purple wildflowers. The margaritas flowed; Miami noticed Ava working her way through a third one.

Miami told Dino, "Any wedding that has a party like this…before the wedding even starts…is my kind of party." He looked at Ava. She looked stunning while being photographed with the other bridesmaids. "I better be careful with this filly," he confided to his friend.

"The Las Vegas futures odds are dropping fast on your single days," said Dino.

Margaritas and pictures continued until 4:00 p.m., when everyone retreated to their rooms to get ready for the ceremony.

At 5:45 p.m. the sun was still high in the west when the seven-man mariachi band members began playing and singing. It sounded as if the band wanted to produce relaxing background music for the wedding, but they just weren't made for it, especially with three trumpet players adding lively input, as the guests were seated. Don Bernie walked his mother to the front row and watched Isabel's mother be led to her seat by a handsome, heavy-set, young brother of the bride.

The ocean's evening coolness was setting in as Miami and Dino, wearing white tuxedos without bow ties, walked with bridesmaids Ava and Amalia in their red strapless dresses to the front of the room. The band was eager to play the familiar "Wedding March" tune with the trumpet players again taking a spirited lead. It was a unique version that set a happy tone.

Isabel's father, looking dark, suave, and impeccably groomed in a black tuxedo appeared arm-in-arm with the bride. Isabel was dressed in a flowing white gown with subtle colored flowers embroidered on the upper portion of the dress. She was not tall, maybe 10 years younger than Bernie, with perfect skin and a pretty, round face, with fresh flowers in her hair. When she smiled at her father, and then at Don Bernie, it was a smile filled with love, warmth, and happiness.

Miami and Don Bernie exchanged a long look, a smile, and a nod. Tears of happiness could be seen in the corners of Big Bernie's eyes.

The room was filled with colors. The room was filled with winners.

At a barn far away, in a comfortable corner stall, stood Winning Colors. She looked out at wide, green meadows, pawed the ground, and waited to run again.

A $1,000,000 Score

Winning Colors Kentucky Derby -Photo Finish (Photo by Bettman)

Mexican Federal Police Forces (Photo by Frontpage)

Zeta Magazine Coverage of Narco Trafficking

Saratoga Race Track (Photo by Barbara Livingston)

Miami Paul - Tijuana, Mexico

Wayne Lukas (Photo by Barbara Livingston)

Santa Anita Race Track (Photo by Cheryl Ann Quigley)

Ava Bouchon and Miami Paul

Miami Paul - 1988

Zeta Magazine Continuing Coverage of El Gato's Murder

LAS VEGAS (Photo by Claudio Zaccherini)

Jockey Gary Stevens (Photo by Cheryl Ann Quigley)

Jeff Lukas and Wayne Lukas 1988 (Photo by Barbara Livingston)

Churchill Downs Kentucky Derby Day (Photo by Barbara Livingston)

Miami Paul - Praying at Race book - Las Vegas, Nevada

Miami Paul - Los Angeles 1988

Map Route - San Diego to Agua Caliente Racetrack

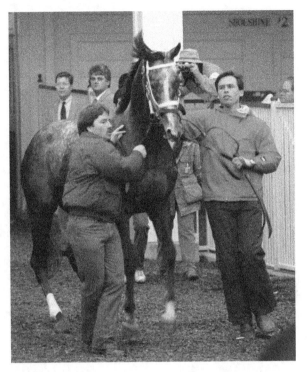

Winning Colors 1988 (Photo by Barbara Livingston)

Saratoga Race Track (Photo by Barbara Livingston)

ACKNOWLEDGEMENTS

Grateful acknowledgment is given for the contributions of Dino Mateo, Ken Stovitz, David Freehling, Rusty Weber, Richard Zien, Stephan Tow, Rick Edwards, Howard Parelskin, Joel Adelman, Steven Semprevivo, Chris Powel, George Vasquez, Robert Robotti, and my mentor and first editor Mary L. Holden.

A special thanks is in order for jockey Gary Stevens and his wife Angie who allowed me to interview them. They both added much detail and color to this story.

For inspiration, I thank author Laura Hillenbrand for writing *Seabiscuit*— the greatest book about horses and racing ever written.

I thank my wife Renee, for without her enthusiasm this book would never have been completed.

BIBLIOGRAPHY

Books

Beltran, David Jimenez. *The Agua Caliente Story: Remembering Mexico's Legendary Racetrack*. Eclipse Press, 2004.

Basave, Daniel Salinas. *La liturgia del tigre blanco: Una leyenda llamada Jorge Hank Rhon*. Océano, 2013.

Bossinakis, Christina. *Sermon On The Mount*. Lukas Enterprises, 2019.

Devito, Carlo. *D.Wayne: The High-Rolling and Fast Times of America's Premier Horse Trainer*. McGraw-Hill Education, 2003.

Hillenbrand, Laura. *Seabiscuit: An American Legend*. Random House, 2001.

Kaufman, Mervyn; Stevens, Gary. *The Perfect Ride*: Gary Stevens. Citadel Press Books, 2002.

Klein, Gene. *First Down and a Billion: The Funny Business of Pro Football*. William Morrow & Company, Inc., 1987.

Magazines (Print and Digital)

BloodHorse
Daily Racing Form
Harvard Business Review
Proceso
Sports Illustrated

All of the following magazine and newspaper website references were accessed between November 26, 2018, and December 9, 2018.

Editor. "Animal Blood." *Proceso*. May 6, 2006. Web. https://translate.google.com/translate?hl=en&sl=es&u=http://www.proceso.com.mx/97248/sangre-animal&prev=search

Johnson, J. Keeler. "Legends: Derby Filly Winning Colors." *BloodHorse*. March 3, 2016. Web. www.bloodhorse.com/horse-racing/articles/209906/legends-derby-filly-winning-colors

Kirby, Julia. "Passion for Detail." *Harvard Business Review*. May 2004. Web. www.hbr.org/2004/05/passion-for-detail

Nack, William. "Another View from the Top," *Sports Illustrated* Vault. May 9, 1988. Web. https://www.si.com/vault/1988/05/09/117615/another-view-from-the-top-just-four-years-ago-gene-klein-fled-the-nfl-and-lit-into-racing-with-a-daring-strategy-and-a-big-bankroll-now-hes-americas-most-successful-owner-of-thoroughbreds

Nack, William, "Lady's Day," *Sports Illustrated* Vault. May 16, 1988. Web. www.si.com/vault/1988/05/16/117677/ladys-day-churchill-downs-rocked-as-the-filly-winning-colors-rolled-over-16-colts-to-triumph-in-the-kentucky-derby

Privman, Jay. "Thirty years after Winning Colors Lukas still in with a shot." *Daily Racing Form*. April 30, 2018. Web. www.drf.com/news/thirty-years-after-winning-colors-lukas-still-shot

Ranft, Patricia. "Horse of a Winning Color." *Kentucky Monthly*. Web. http://www.kentuckymonthly.com/lifestyle/featured/horse-of-a-winning-color/

Newspapers (Print and Digital)

Agencia Fronteriza De Noticias
Frontline/PBS
KentuckyDerby.com
LAWEEKLY.com
Los Angeles Times
Mexico Perspective
New York Times
Proyecto Impunidad: Crímenes Contra Periodistas
Reuters
San Diego Reader
Sinembargo
Vanguardia
Washington Post
Zeta

Cortéz, Dora Elena. "That April 20 ..." *Agencia Fronteriza De Noticias*. April 30, 2015. Web. https://translate.google.com/translate?hl=en&sl=es&u=http://www.afntijuana.info/afn_politico/40110_aquel_20_de_abril&prev=search

Bergman, Lowell. "Family tree: The Hanks." *Frontline*. 2000. Web. https://www.pbs.org/wgbh/pages/frontline/shows/mexico/family/bergman.html

KentuckyDerby.com "Attendance/On-Track Handle/All Sources Handle." 2018. https://www.kentuckyderby.com/uploads/wysiwyg/assets/uploads/Attendance___Handle_-_Top__2018_.pdf

Kun, Josh. "The Island of Jorge Hank Rhon." *LAWEEKLY*. Feb. 15, 2006. Web. https://www.laweekly.com/news/the-island-of-jorge-hank-rhon-2141922

Horstman, Barry M., Distel, Dave. "Ex-Charger Owner Klein Dead at 69." Los Angeles Times. March 13, 1990. Web. http://articles.latimes.com/1990-03-13/sports/sp-260_1_san-diego-chargers

McDonnell, Patrick. "Gunmen Kill Satiric Tijuana Columnist." *Los Angeles Times*. April 21, 1988. Web. http://articles.latimes.com/1988-04-21/local/me-2291_1_tijuana-street

McDonnell, Patrick. "Fugitive Held in Tijuana Writer's Death: Crime: The ex-security chief at Caliente Racetrack, captured in L.A., is back in Mexico to face charges in the slaying of the columnist known as El Gato." *Los Angeles Times*. May 3, 1990. Web. http://articles.latimes.com/1990-05-03/local/me-67_1_el-gato

Rohter, Larry. "Tijuana Journal; 'The Cat' Clawed Many; Is One His Murderer?" *New York Times*. July 1, 1988. Web. https://www.nytimes.com/1988/07/01/world/tijuana-journal-the-cat-clawed-many-is-one-his-murderer.html

"Gene Klein, 69, Sold N.F.L. Club And Later Owned Derby Winner." *New York Times*. March 13, 1990. Web. https://www.nytimes.com/1990/03/13/obituaries/gene-klein-69-sold-nfl-club-and-later-owned-derby-winner.html

"Héctor Felix Miranda, Mexico." Proyecto Impunidad. April 20, 1988. Web. http://www.impunidad.com/caso.php?id=72&idioma=us

Diaz, Lizbeth. "Flamboyant ex-mayor arrested with arsenal in Mexico." *Reuters World News*. June 4, 2011. Web. https://www.reuters.com/article/us-mexico-arrest/flamboyant-ex-mayor-arrested-with-arsenal-in-mexico-idUSTRE7531TV20110605

Matthews, Neal. "Jorge Hank Rhon finally talks." *San Diego Reader*. May 10, 1990. Web. https://www.sandiegoreader.com/news/1990/may/10/cover-jorge-hank-finally-talks/

Navarro, Adela; García, Inés. "Asesino del periodista "El Gato" Félix sale libre y acude a su ex patrón: Jorge Hank Rhon." *Sinembargo*. May 12, 2015. www.sinembargo.mx/12-05-2015/1342606

Martinez, Jose M. "'El Gato' Felix and Jorge Hank Rhon, 25 years of impunity." *Vanguardia.mx*. March 12, 2012. Web. https://www.vanguardia.com.mx/columnas-elgatofelixyjorgehankrhon25anosdeimpunidad-1238894.html

Carl, Traci. "Colorful Tijuana Mayor in Mexico Race." *The Associated Press*: *Washington Post*. August 2, 2007. Web. http://www.washingtonpost.com/wp-dyn/content/article/2007/08/02/AR2007080201536_pf.html?noredirect=on

Bever, Lindsey; Robinson, Lynda. "'My Old Kentucky Home': The Kentucky Derby's beloved, fraught singalong about slavery." *The Washington Post*. May 5, 2018. Web. https://www.washingtonpost.com/news/retropolis/wp/2018/05/05/my-old-kentucky-home-the-kentucky-derbys-beloved-fraught-sing-along-about-slavery/?utm_term=.336b23f7df68

"El Gato." *ZetaTijuana*.com. April 20, 2014. Web. http://Zetatijuana.com/2014/04/el-gato/

YouTube and Other Videos

"1988 Santa Anita Derby" 3.19 minutes. TheXvid. April 9,1988. https://thexvid.com/video/rmLhZy37BAM/1988-santa-anita-derby.html

"1988 Kentucky Derby." 2.28 minutes. YouTube. January 1, 2008. www.youtube.com/watch?v=maKjghSxcAI

"D. Wayne Lukas for the Kentucky Derby Museum." 2.51 minutes. YouTube. May 8, 2017. www.youtube.com/watch?v=Un_jyhIozQ4

"1988 Kentucky Derby - Winning Colors: Full Broadcast." 1:07:53 minutes. YouTube. April 25, 2012. https://www.youtube.com/watch?v=L59bowqEBl4

Twitter

@DRFPrivman. "RLT, Lukas watched Derby in a small alcove just off the tunnel that leads from paddock to the track, on a small television. 'I don't know how you'll watch the race on that,' a reporter shadowing Lukas commented. 'She's gray. And she'll be in front the whole way,' he replied." Twitter, April 30, 2018, 12:35 p.m., https://twitter.com/DRFPrivman/status/991038436676169734

Photo Description

Image #1 $1,000,000 In Vault

Image #2   BET:514700076 Kentucky Derby Victory

Image #3   Closeup of a handgun of Mexican federal police forces maintaining order in the violent border city of Ciudad Juarez

Image #4   Zeta Magazine Coverage of Narco Trafficking

Image #5   Saratoga 2002

Image #6   Miami Paul - Tijuana, Mexico

Image #7   Wayne Lukas, Hall of Fame trainer, at Saratoga in 1989

Image #8   A field of thoroughbreds rounds the far turn in a race at historic Santa Anita Park on Feb 10, 2010

Image #9   Ava Bouchon and Miami Paul

Image #10   Miami Paul - 1988

Image #11   Zeta Magazine Continuing Coverage of El Gato's Murder

Image #12   LAS VEGAS – JUNE 22, 1979

Image #13   Jockey Gary Stevens Before Winning the Frank E. Kilroe Mile, Santa Anita Racetrack, 3/6/04

Image #14   Jeff Lukas and Wayne Lukas 1988

Image #15   Churchill Downs Twin Spires Roses Kentucky Derby Day

Image #16   Miami Paul - Praying at Race book - Las Vegas, Nevada

Image #17   Miami Paul - Los Angeles Pink Cadillac 1988

Image #18   "THE ROAD TO HELL" - Agua Caliente Race Track - Tijuana - (Google Maps)

Image #19   Winning Colors with Kiaran McLaughlin and Jeff Lukas, 1988 Breeders' Cup Distaff

Image #20   Horseracing scene Thoroughbreds at Saratoga Race Course 2004

ABOUT THE AUTHOR

Mark Paul lives for action and adventure at locations where gambling occurs. While racing motorcycles at age 15, he was incarcerated in a Mexican jail (he was released after six days, completely rehabilitated). He began his gambling career by sneaking into Hollywood Park and Santa Anita at age 16. Mark made a 5,000-mile journey in a sailboat through the Panama Canal, and then on to the island of Jamaica, to attend Caribbean and South American horseraces. He completed these gambling junkets alone, via bus, to gamble at the local thoroughbred racetracks. He was a participant in a million-dollar win on the 1988 Kentucky Derby with two other gamblers through a bet placed in Tijuana, Mexico. He has owned interests in 34 racehorses. Mark enjoyed a long career in commercial real estate. With his wife, Renee, Mark raised over $750,000 for City of Hope cancer research through their events held at the Santa Anita racetrack.

www.markpaulauthor.com

CPSIA information can be obtained
at www.ICGtesting.com
Printed in the USA
LVHW011036130720
660476LV00004B/255

9 781949 642285